Spiritual Assessment: A Handbook for Helping Professionals

David R. Hodge, Ph.D.

NORTH AMERICAN ASSOCIATION OF CHRISTIANS IN SOCIAL WORK

Botsford, CT 06404 www.nacsw.org

Copyright 2003 by:
North American Association of Christians in Social Work
PO Box 121
Botsford, CT 06404
www.nacsw.org

Edited by: Diana Garland
Design: Rick Chamiec-Case
Cover Design and Cover Photograph: Linda Champanier

IBSN: 0-9715318-0-3

CONTENTS

CHAPTER 1

Introduction

This short, practice-oriented text is designed to equip helping professionals conduct spiritual assessments. Toward this end, this book collects a number of assessment tools that have been published in different journals and places them in the hands of helping professionals in one convenient format. In addition to being of interest to social workers, this text should be of use to psychologists, nurses, pastors and other helping professionals interested in spiritual assessment.

Indeed, a growing consensus exists across disciplines regarding the importance of spiritual assessment. Increasingly helping professionals (Canda & Furman, 1999), academics (Plante & Sharma, 2001) and accrediting organizations acknowledge the importance of spiritual assessment. The Joint Commission on Accreditation of Healthcare Organizations (JCAHO), for example, now recommends that a spiritual assessment be undertaken with clients (JCAHO, 2002).

Many reasons underlie this emerging consensus. Four factors, however, seem particularly important: the need to understand clients' worldviews in order to provide effective services, respect for clients' autonomy, the emergence of the strengths perspective, and the importance of grounding practice in professional ethics. I briefly review these reasons below.

Why Conduct a Spiritual Assessment?

As mentioned above, there are at least four reasons why it is important to consider conducting a spiritual assessment. First, to provide effective, client-centered services, it is critical for helping professionals to develop some understanding of clients' basic worldviews. For many individuals, spirituality is central to their understanding of themselves and the world around them. Religion is the vehicle through which spirituality is commonly expressed (Pargament, 1997). Approximately a third of the general population in the United States considers religion to be the most important dimension of their lives (Gallup & Lindsay, 1999;

Walsh, 1999). Other surveys indicate that religion plays a role of increased salience for many populations of interest to helping professionals, such as African Americans, Hispanics, women, the elderly and people who are poor (Davis & Robinson, 1997; Gallup & Lindsay, 1999; Pargament, 1997).

In short, for many clients, it is necessary to understand their spirituality in order to understand their worldviews. At a practical level, clients' spiritual worldviews can affect attitudes and practices in a number of areas, including attitudes and practices about animals, child care, diet, marital relations, medical care, military participation, recreation, schooling and many other areas of significance to helping professionals (Rey, 1997).

For instance, as an expression of their spirituality, some Muslims consider dogs unclean. Evangelical Christians commonly affirm holistic child care practices that combine structure and discipline with nurture and affection. Orthodox Jews tend to follow a kosher dietary protocol. In contrast to the egalitarian marital model affirmed by the dominant secular cultural, Mormons widely affirm complementary marriages.

If helping professionals hold biased understandings of clients' spiritual beliefs and values in these and other areas, it can damage the client/practitioner relationship (Koenig, 1998; Richards & Bergin, 1997; Richards & Bergin, 2000). Helping professionals who believe in the innate superiority of egalitarian marriages, for example, may have trouble working with Mormon clients, especially if they do not understand the strengths complementary marriages typically provide Mormon couples. To provide effective, client-centered services, helping professionals must have an unbiased, culturally sensitive understanding of clients' spiritual worldviews (Reddy & Hanna, 1998; Rey, 1997; Robbins, Chatterjee & Canda, 1998). Conducting a spiritual assessment allows helping professions a method of understanding clients' spiritual worldviews and how those worldviews relate to the provision of services.

The second reason underscoring the importance of a spiritual assessment is respect for client self-determination. As noted immediately above, for many clients, spirituality is central to their belief system. Because of the pivotal nature of these beliefs, many individuals desire to have their spiritual beliefs and values integrated into counseling settings (Privette, Quackenbos & Bundrick, 1994). According to Gallup data reported by Bart (1998), 66% of the public would prefer to see a professional counselor with spiritual values and beliefs, while 81% wanted to have their own values and beliefs integrated into the counseling process. In order to integrate clients' spiritual beliefs and values into the therapeutic process, helping professionals must have some knowledge of what those beliefs and values are. If practitioners do not understand clients' spiritual worldviews, then they may have difficulty respecting clients' desire to incorporate their spiritual beliefs and values into the counseling dialogue. Spiritual assessment provides a means to elicit clients' spiritual beliefs and values so that they can be integrated into the therapeutic process.

The third rationale for considering a spiritual assessment is the growing interest in using clients' strengths to address problems. In tandem with other helping professions, social work has shown increased interest in using clients' strengths to overcome problems (Saleebey, 1997; Saleebey, 2000). Even helping professionals who are not strict adherents of the strengths perspective frequently highlight the importance of utilizing clients' strengths to address problems. A growing body of research indicates that spirituality is often a significant strength (Ellison & Levin, 1998; Gartner, 1996; George, Larson, Koenig & McCullough, 2000; Koenig, McCullough & Larson, 2001; Larson, et al., 1992; Pargament, 1997; Ventis, 1995). Further, evidence suggests that the salience of spirituality frequently becomes more prominent during difficult times (Ferraro & Kelley-Moore, 2000; Pargament, 1997).

In order to operationalize clients' strengths, helping professionals must have some understanding of the strengths that animate their clients' lives. Conducting a spiritual assessment provides a framework for eliciting clients' spiritual strengths.

The fourth reason for considering a spiritual assessment is derived from ethical stipulations propagated in professional codes of ethics. Professional codes of ethics typically suggest that helping professionals are ethically obligated to engage in spiritually competent practice. To cite one example, the Code of Ethics of the National Association of Social Work (NASW) (1999) lists four standards (1.05c, 2.01b, 4.02 and 6.04d) that explicitly mention religion as a category toward which social workers should strive to exhibit sensitivity. Similarly, the NASW Code of Ethics lists at least two standards (1.05a, 1.05b) that implicitly mention religion as a category toward which social workers should strive to exhibit sensitivity.

More specifically, social workers are ethically compelled to obtain education about religious diversity and the oppression religious peoples encounter in various forums (1.05 c), avoid unwarranted negative criticism and derogatory language based upon religion (2.01 b; c.f. 1.12), refrain from facilitating any form of religious discrimination (4.02), and actively work to prevent and eliminate religious discrimination (6.04d). Since people of faith comprise distinct cultural groups based upon the norms of their spiritual worldviews (Fellin, 2000; Talbot, 2000), social workers should also recognize the strengths that exist in faith-based cultures (1.05a) and demonstrate competence and sensitivity in their service provision to such groups (1.05b).

It is difficult to comply with these ethical stipulations without some knowledge of clients' spiritual beliefs and values. It is, for example, difficult to exhibit spiritual competency and sensitivity to clients' spiritual cultures if one has no knowledge of clients' spiritual beliefs and values. It is comparatively easy to engage in practices that exhibit bias toward a client's spiritual worldview if one has no knowledge of that worldview. In short, conducting a spiritual assessment enables helping professionals to comply with common ethical standards.

I have briefly reviewed four rationales for considering a spiritual assessment—understanding clients' worldviews, respecting clients' autonomy, eliciting clients' spiritual strengths, and grounding one's practice in professional ethics. While considerable overlap exists among these four reasons, they serve to highlight the importance of spiritual assessments. With these rationales in mind, I now turn to providing an overview of the five assessment tools that comprise the core of this handbook.

Overview of assessment instruments

The following five chapters consist of different assessment instruments that have been previously published as separate articles in various social science journals. These five discrete assessment tools were developed as a series. In other words, the instruments are designed to be complementary. Each assessment instrument has its own unique set of strengths that suggest its use in different settings.

This handbook gathers these five discrete tools together in one location for the first time. Helping professionals can thus acquaint themselves with different approaches to spiritual assessment and chose the instrument that best fits the client's needs in a given situation. Instead of relying upon a one-size-fits-all approach to assessment, helping professionals can develop a "toolbox" of various assessment approaches, selecting the appropriate assessment tool for the job at hand. Directly below, I briefly review the following five chapters, each of which profiles a different assessment approach. In addition to introducing the reader to the assessment instruments, I also touch on some of the strengths that are unique to each spiritual assessment tool.

Chapter Two begins by reviewing common assessment approaches and then transitions into a delineation of a verbal spiritual history. This method, which is analogous to conducting a family history, appears to be the most widely used approach to spiritual assessment. It may particularly appeal to verbally oriented clients and provides an opportunity for the practitioner to join with the client via the process of conducting a verbally based assessment. This approach, which as stated above is verbal, stands in contrast to the following assessment methods, which are pictorial.

The assessment tool depicted in Chapter Three is a spiritual lifemap. This diagrammatic instrument is similar to a verbal spiritual history in that it charts or "maps" a client's spiritual journey on a large sheet of paper. This approach may appeal to more artistically oriented clients as well as those who may be uncomfortable discussing what is a very intimate, personal topic. Spiritual lifemaps can also be easily explained, assigned as homework, and then discussed at a later date when they are completed. As is the case with all pictorial instruments, the concrete delineation of clients' strengths helps to reinforce their existence in clients' lives.

Chapter Four describes a spiritual ecomap. The spiritual ecomap depicts a client's relationships with various spiritual entities that exist in the present environment. In a manner similar to traditional ecomaps, spiritual ecomaps focus on current, existential relationships to entities that are often sources of present strength. In contrast to the above approaches, spiritual ecomaps focus on the "here-and-now," or on clients' relationships in space. Accordingly, spiritual ecomaps may be particularly well suited for work with clients who are interested in focusing on how present assets can be marshaled to address current problems. In addition, spiritual ecomaps may be the quickest assessment approach to complete.

Chapter Five discusses the process of creating a spiritual genogram. In a manner analogous to traditional genograms, spiritual genograms chart the flow of spirituality across at least three generations. In contrast to the above tools, spiritual genograms allow clients to see how their spiritual heritage has shaped their present reality. This method may be particularly useful when working with couples, in situations where the extended family plays a significant role in the life of the client, and in contexts where it is helpful to understand clients' spiritual history across time.

The spiritual ecogram is profiled in Chapter Six. Drawing elements from both spiritual ecomaps and spiritual genograms, this tool depicts clients' spirituality in present space and across time. In other words, this method delineates clients' present relationships with spiritual entities while concurrently depicting the flow of spirituality across three generations. In addition, the connections between past and present functioning are also displayed upon the diagrammatic instrument. This instrument may be particularly useful when the situation calls for an understanding of past and present relationships and their interconnections.

This overview provides a brief orientation to the following chapters. Readers should feel free to skip over material that seems redundant; picking and choosing from the chapters as best suits their individual needs. The text concludes with a brief chapter on spiritual competency and lists some resources for further study. As mentioned above, the next chapter begins by reviewing the present state of qualitative assessment instruments and introducing a model for conducting a verbally based spiritual history.

References

Bart, M. (1998). Spirituality in counseling finding believers. *Counseling Today, 41*(6), 1, 6.

Canda, E. R., & Furman, L. D. (1999). *Spiritual diversity in social work practice.* New York: The Free Press.

Davis, N. J., & Robinson, R. V. (1997). A war for America's soul? The American religious landscape. In R. H. Williams (Ed.), *Cultural wars in American politics* (pp. 39-61). New York: Aldine De Gruyter.

Ellison, C. G., & Levin, J. S. (1998). The religion-health

connection: Evidence, theory, and future directions. *Health Education and Behavior, 25*(6), 700-720.

Fellin, P. (2000). Revisiting multiculturalism in social work. *Journal of Social Work Education, 36*(2), 261-278.

Ferraro, K. F., & Kelley-Moore, J. A. (2000). Religious consolation among men and women: Do health problems spur seeking? *Journal of the Scientific Study of Religion, 39*(2), 220-234.

Gallup, G. J., & Lindsay, D. M. (1999). *Surveying the religious landscape.* Harrisburg, PA: Morehouse Publishing.

Gartner, J. D. (1996). Religious commitment, mental health, and prosocial behavior: A review of the empirical literature. In E. P. Shafranske (Ed.), *Religion and the clinical practice of psychology* (pp. 187-214). Washington, DC: American Psychological Association.

George, L. K., Larson, D. B., Koenig, H. G., & McCullough, M. E. (2000). Spirituality and health: What we know, what we need to know. *Journal of Social and Clinical Psychology, 19*(1), 102-116.

JCAHO. (2002). Spiritual assessment. In Standards - Frequently asked questions [Online]. Available: http://www.jcaho.org/standard/pharmfaq_mpfrm.html (Accessed 21/03/02).

Koenig, H. G., McCullough, M. E., & Larson, D. B. (2001). *Handbook of religion and health.* New York: Oxford University Press.

Koenig, H., G. (Editor). (1998). *Handbook of religion and mental health.* New York: Academic Press.

Larson, D. B., Sherriall, K. A., Lyons, J. S., Craigie Jr, F. C., Thielman, S. B., Greenwold, M. A., & Larson, S. S. (1992). Associations between dimensions of religious commitment and mental health reported in the American Journal of Psychiatry and Archives of General Psychiatry: 1978-1989. *American Journal of Psychiatry, 149*(4), 557-559.

NASW Code of Ethics. (1999). Available: www.naswdc.org/Code/ethics.htm (Accessed 1/20/00).

Pargament, K. I. (1997). *The psychology of religion and coping.* New York: Guilford Press.

Plante, T. G., & Sharma, N. K. (2001). Religious faith and mental health outcomes. In T. G. Plante & A. C. Sherman (Eds.), *Faith and health* (pp. 240-261). New York: Guilford Press.

Privette, G., Quackenbos, S., & Bundrick, C. M. (1994). Preferences for religious and nonreligious counseling and psychotherapy. *Psychological Reports, 75,* 539-547.

Reddy, I., & Hanna, F. J. (1998). The lifestyle of the Hindu women: Conceptualizing female clients from Indian origin. *The Journal of Individual Psychology, 54*(3), 384-398.

Rey, L. D. (1997). Religion as invisible culture: Knowing about and knowing with. *Journal of Family Social Work, 2*(2), 159-177.

Richards, P. S., & Bergin, A. E. (1997). *A spiritual strategy.* Washington, DC: American Psychological Association.

Richards, P. S., & Bergin, A. E. (Eds.). (2000). *Handbook of psychotherapy and religious diversity.* Washington, DC: American Psychological Association.

Robbins, S. P., Chatterjee, P., & Canda, E. R. (1998). *Contemporary human behavior theory.* Boston: Allyn & Bacon.

Saleebey, D. (Editor). (1997). *The strengths perspective in social work practice* (2nd ed.). White Plains, NY: Longman.

Saleebey, D. (2000). Power in the people: Strengths and hope. *Advances in Social Work, 1*(2), 127-136.

Talbot, M. (2000, February 27). A mighty fortress. *The New York Times Magazine,* 34-41, 66-8, 84-5.

Ventis, W. L. (1995). The relationship between religion and mental health. *Journal of Social Issues, 51*(2), 33-48.

Walsh, F. (1999). Religion and spirituality. In F. Walsh (Ed.), *Spiritual resources in family therapy* (pp. 3-27). New York: Gilford Press.

CHAPTER TWO

Spiritual Histories: A Verbally-Based Approach to Spiritual Assessment[1]

Assessment tends to be an underdeveloped area in social work, and likely other professions as well (Mattaini & Kirk, 1991). Nowhere is the lack of maturation more evident than in spiritual assessment tools (Bullis, 1996; Sherwood, 1998). While there have been numerous calls for the reintegration of spirituality into the therapeutic dialogue (Bullis, 1996; Cornett, 1992; Derezotes, 1995; Hodge, 1998; Jacobs, 1997; Poole, 1998; Rey, 1997; Sermabeikian, 1994), multidimensional frameworks that assess spirituality in a therapeutically constructive fashion are conspicuously absent. Surveys have repeatedly shown that social workers, for example, have received little training in issues related to spirituality, including assessment (Bullis, 1996; Derezotes, 1995; Sheridan, Bullis, Adcock, Berlin & Miller, 1992; Furman & Chandy, 1994). More specifically, Furman and Chandy (1994) found that over three quarters of practitioners received little or no training in spirituality during their graduate education, in spite of the central role it plays in the lives of many clients.

Spurring interest in the assessment of spirituality has been the accumulation of an impressive body of empirical findings documenting spirituality's salience in a wide range of areas, including: mental health (Ventis, 1995), coping ability (Pargament, 1997), self-esteem (Ellison, 1993), and the realization of personal strengths (Maton & Salem, 1995). It is also a significant variable in recovery from divorce (Nathanson, 1995), homelessness (Montgomery, 1994), sexual assault (Kennedy, Davis & Talyor, 1998), and substance abuse (Muffler, Langrod & Larson, 1992). In total,

---

[1] Much of the material in this chapter appeared previously in an article written by D. R. Hodge entitled, "Spiritual assessment: A review of major qualitative methods and a new framework for assessing spirituality" (2001). *Social Work*, 43(3), 203-214. It is used in this book with the permission of NASW.

several hundred studies exist on spirituality and religion, the majority of which suggest that spirituality is a key strength in personal well-being (Ellison & Levin, 1998). While spirituality and religion are often used interchangeably, they are distinct, although overlapping, concepts (Carroll, 1997). Religion flows from spirituality and expresses an internal subjective reality, corporately, in particular institutionalized forms, rituals, beliefs and practices (Canda, 1997; Carroll, 1997). Accordingly, spirituality is defined as a relationship with God (or whatever is held to be the Ultimate or Transcendent, e.g. a set of sacred texts for Buddhists) that fosters a sense of meaning, purpose and mission in life. In turn, this relationship produces fruit, such as altruism, love, forgiveness, etc. which has a discernible effect upon one's relationship to self, nature, others, and the Ultimate (Carroll, 1997; Sermabeikian, 1994; Spero, 1990).

An additional factor stimulating interest in assessing spirituality is a growing acceptance among helping professionals of what is widely referred to as the strengths perspective. This framework posits clients' personal and environmental strengths as central to the helping process. With growing utilization of clients' capabilities in the clinical dialogue to ameliorate problems, interest in how to identify clients' strengths, such as spirituality, has increased (Cowger, 1994; Hwang, Cowger & Saleebey, 1998).

Assessment is critical to the incorporation of strengths into the therapeutic milieu. As Ronnau and Poertner (1993) noted, without a reliable means for finding clients' strengths, practitioners tend to revert to practice models that are based upon the identification of problems and deficits. Further, in addition to identification, strengths must be organized into a conceptual framework that suggests particular interventions. As Rauch (1993) observed, gathering data is not an assessment in itself. It must be interpreted, organized, integrated with theory and made meaningful. Accordingly, assessment is defined as the process of gathering, analyzing and synthesizing salient data into a multidimensional formulation that provides the basis for action decisions (Rauch, 1993).

Quantitative vs. Qualitative Assessment Instruments

The most widely used spiritual assessment tools are quantitative measures, or pen and paper questionnaires (Lukoff, Turner & Lu, 1993). Quantitative assessment methods in general, however, have been criticized (Franklin & Jordan, 1995; Rodman, 1987; Scott, 1989). This perspective argues that quantitative instruments presuppose a certain construction of reality and in the process leave little room for clients to negotiate a shared understanding of their individual experience with practitioners. The subjective, often intangible, nature of human existence is left uncaptured. Potentially vital information can be lost as clients circumscribe their experiences to fit the limited options presented in a specific scale and its predetermined understanding of reality.

The problems inherent in quantitative assessment may be particularly relevant in the realm of spirituality. Reed (1992), for instance, has argued that spirituality, as a subjective interior reality, is difficult to quantify in any manner. Further, this reality can vary radically across various spiritual traditions (e.g., feminist goddess traditions vs. Islamic traditions) making attempts at quantification difficult (Robbins, Chatterjee & Canda, 1998).

A further practical issue is the low levels of education that exist among many of the populations for whom spirituality is especially salient. For example, George (1997) reported that approximately 20% of the current cohort of elderly adults is functionally illiterate. The sophisticated vocabulary and complex questions in many quantitative measures increase the probability of incorrect responses and can foster a dynamic that mitigates against the formation of a therapeutic alliance.

Accordingly, spirituality seems better served by qualitative assessment methods. Qualitative approaches tend to be holistic, open ended, individualistic, ideographic, and process oriented (Franklin & Jordan, 1995). As such they offer particular strengths in terms of assessing clients' spiritual reality where richness of information can be of particular importance (Mattaini & Kirk, 1993). Further, depending upon the method used, they can foster a collaborative, strengths-based atmosphere (Hartman, 1995).

Qualitative Assessment Approaches

According to Ed Canda, a widely acknowledge expert on spirituality in the field of social work, a limited number of qualitative assessment methods currently exist (personal communication, April 22, 1998). One of the more prominent approaches is taking a religious/spiritual history (Boyd, 1998; Bullis, 1996; Dombeck & Karl, 1987; O' Rourke, 1997; Peck, 1993; Rizzuto, 1996; Tan, 1996). This process is analogous to taking a family history. The client and practitioner work together to explore the religious tradition of both parents, the client's spiritual beliefs and practices, along with the degree of integration with the community at large. From the client's perspective, it is important to understand the public (baptism, confirmation, Bar-Mitzvah, rites of passage, membership, etc.) and private (conversions, spiritual awakenings, transpersonal communion, peak experiences, etc.) significance of the family's faith tradition throughout the developmental process. Deviation, if any, from the family's religious orientation is examined, along with the current existential experience of the Transcendent.

Spiritual histories commonly use a series of questions to operationalize the above themes in the context of an empathetic dialogue. An open-ended, co-exploration of the client's spiritual and religious beliefs results. The question sets are often organized in a chronological format. This allows spiritual assessment to occur in an autobiographical/narrative format that is comfortable and natural to the client (Strickland, 1994).

However, some spiritual histories employ an alternative ordering of questions to achieve certain therapeutic ends. For example, Dombeck and Karl (1987, p. 193) offered a framework which organized questions into the following three areas: "placement within a religious community" (e.g. "Religious affiliation?" "Changes in religious affiliation?" "Level of present involvement?"); "personal meanings attached to symbols, rituals, beliefs and Divine figures" (e.g. "What religious practices are most meaningful?" "When and in what ways does one feel close to the Divine?"); and "relationship to religious resources" (e.g. "What is relationship with God?" "How is God involved in your problems?"). This ordering attempts to provide practitioners with a working knowledge of clients' religious traditions, their sociology, practices, key symbols, and unique language, in turn suggesting salutary spiritual interventions based upon clients' religious and spiritual strengths.

As a supplement to histories, diagrammatic instruments, such as spiritual genograms and spiritual maps, provide useful means of organizing data (Bullis, 1996; Rey, 1997). Alternatively, as will be discussed in the following chapters, they can stand on their own as assessment tools.

An instrument related to spiritual histories is Nino's (1997) spiritual quest. Nino suggested using sentence compilations in assessment. Nino (1997, p. 208) offered the following ten items: "1. I see myself now. . ., 2. I think the spiritual. . ., 3. The people I have met. . ., 4. Thinking about my past. . ., 5. When I feel fragmented. . ., 6. My relation to God. . ., 7. The world around me. . ., 8. A meaningful life. . ., 9. The best thing I have ever done. . ., 10. What I would really like to do. . ." This is supplemented by the selection of a time period, or event, in the client's life that can explain the nature and meaning of the statements made above. A more detailed narrative emerges that provides a number of insights into the client's spiritual world.

Pruyser's (1976, p. 60) seven categories for "pastoral diagnosis" have been highly influential in spiritual assessment (Fitchett, 1993). Pruyser suggested seven areas to explore with clients: (1) "Awareness of the Holy:" What does one experience, or hold to be, sacred? (2) "Providence:" How does trust or hope function in the client's life? (3) "Faith:" What does one commit oneself to? (4) "Grace or Gratefulness:" For what is the client thankful? (5) "Repentance:" How does the client handle personal transgressions, or guilt? (6) "Communion:" Who does one feel connected to? (7) "Sense of Vocation:" What sense of purpose is found in life and work? Pruyser advocated listening to clients' stories with the aim of understanding how their narratives relate to these seven themes, using category specific queries as necessary to explore all seven areas.

Fitchett's (1993) 7x7 model places the assessment of seven spiritual dimensions within a broader framework. The intent is to produce a complete assessment that encompasses all bio-psycho-social-spiritual factors relevant to well-being. Fitchette's (1993, p. 42) seven spiritual dimensions are: "beliefs and meaning," "vocation and consequences," "experiences and emotion," "courage and growth," "ritual and practice," "community," and "authority and guidance."

Lovinger (1996) provides a "denominational framework" that consists of an overview of contemporary religious belief systems (e.g. Roman Catholicism; Judaism) through which to understand clients' spiritual narratives. Ten markers of spiritual pathology and five indicators of spiritual maturity are also supplied which can be applied to individuals in any denomination. In total, this yields a framework through which to evaluate clients' current spiritual state.

A number of individuals have proposed stage models for use in practice settings, including assessment (Cowley, 1996; Genia,

1990; Kilpatrick & Holland, 1990; Peck, 1993). In a manner similar to psycho-social stages, these models delineate a series of spiritual developmental stages through which individuals pass. Fowler's (1981) framework, in which individuals move through five sequential stages of faith development, often serves as a foundation for other works in this category and stands as an assessment instrument itself. Regardless of the model, the following approach tends to be used. The client's stage of faith is discerned via a spiritual autobiography, stage specific questions, or a combination of both approaches. Interventions are then targeted to foster advancement to the next stage.

Evaluation of Existing Frameworks

The above review of prominent qualitative approaches is arranged in a specific order. The frameworks explicated above impose generally increasing levels of theoretical structure on the spiritual experience of clients. At one end of the continuum are spiritual histories. While the content and form of questions asked in histories does impose a certain structure on clients' reality (Sermabeikian, 1994), the imposition is minimized by the open-ended, co-exploration of clients' spiritual reality.

At the other end of the continuum are assessment models based upon stage theories that attempt to understand clients' spiritual reality in light of a particular level on a predetermined, sequential series of stages. A number of the concerns that have been raised concerning quantitative assessment can be applied to these latter models due to the similarity of the underlying philosophical assumptions. For instance, just as quantitative instruments imply the need for an "expert clinician" to interpret the measure, stage theories also imply the need for a comparable individual to interpret the client's spiritual state in correspondence with the various stages. Similarly, one particular measure, or one sequential series of stages, is proposed as the true reality for all individuals across diverse spiritual traditions (Robbins, et al., 1998).

Further, there is an increased likelihood that practitioners will slip into a deficit mindset when utilizing stage models as compared to frameworks at the other end of the continuum. Inevitably with stage theories, a certain percentage of clients fall into the lower stages of development. In many cases, these lower stages are characterized by pathological markers. However, in all cases, these individuals are considered less "mature" than those higher up the ladder of development. In short, they are deficient. This understanding of spirituality tends to channel practitioners towards a stance in which deficits predominate in practitioners' interactions with clients. As Saleebey (1992) has observed, when a framework classifies clients pejoratively, labeling them "egocentric" or "dogmatic" (Genia, 1990) or even immature, practitioners will find it difficult to focus on client strengths.

While the latter frameworks have the advantage of suggesting specific interventions, concurrently, as noted above, there are a number of liabilities associated with their use in clinical settings. Conversely, open-ended spiritual histories maximize client autonomy. These frameworks, however, have also been criticized for failing to yield information of sufficient depth and detail (Sperry & Giblin, 1996). While stage theories imply interventions (i.e., to move clients to the next stage), current versions of spiritual histories frequently offer practitioners little in the way of specific suggested interventions.

Accordingly, the rest of this chapter provides an assessment method that combines the strengths of existing qualitative assessment frameworks. It maximizes client autonomy by utilizing the format of a spiritual history while providing the practitioner with an interpretive framework for eliciting information and integrating the resulting information. In turn, this framework suggests specific interventions.

A Spiritual Anthropology

The starting point in developing such an assessment framework is articulating a spiritual anthropology. As Bullis (1996, p. 40) observed, "it is the anthropology that drives the methodology of a spiritual . . . assessment and intervention." It provides the theoretical framework that implies the gathering of certain information and how the resulting data is understood. This process then suggests particular interventions.

Chinese spirituality writer Watchman Nee (1968) conceptualizes the human spirit as an integrative unity comprised of communion, conscience, and intuition. All three dimensions interact with and influence one another along with affect, cognition and volition. As with affect, cognition and volition, the three dimensions can be defined individually.

Communion refers to relationship. More specifically, it refers to the capacity to bond and relate with God (Nee, 1968). In many spiritual traditions, communion is manifested primarily in terms of a relationship with a supreme being (e.g. Allah in Islam, Jesus in Christian Evangelicalism, God in Sikhism). In other traditions, however, the central emphasis may be upon one's relationship to the creation (certain Native American traditions), the transcendent aspect of the self (New Age), or a sacred text (Buddhism).

Conscience can be defined as one's subjective ethical guidance system (Nee, 1968). Beyond one's cognitively held beliefs and values, it informs regarding what is just and fair. It can be thought of as an individual's most deeply held value system.

Intuition is associated with knowledge. More specifically, insights arrive at one's conscious level directly, by-passing normal information process channels (Nee, 1968). Krill (1990) suggests intuition is the process of drawing upon a reservoir of integrated understanding within ourselves. Hunches concerning the advisability of a specific course of action, sudden impressions to pray for someone, creative flashes of insight, are examples of the intuitive function of the spirit (Nee, 1968).

A Framework for Spiritual Assessment

A spiritual assessment framework is provided in Table 1 (see pg. 21). There is a considerable amount of evidence that information is stored and organized narratively in the mind (Strickland, 1994). Accordingly, The Initial Narrative Framework provides three general question categories to foster an autobiographical spiritual history. The question categories are essentially chronological and incorporate increasing levels of personal revelation. This allows time for the practitioner to establish trust and rapport in the helping relationship before more intimate information is shared, an important concern given that spirituality is an intensely private, and therefore sensitive, area for many clients (Krill, 1990).

To facilitate trust, care should be taken to foster a relaxed, conversational atmosphere that mitigates the power differential inherent in therapy (Laird, 1994). For example, moving from behind one's desk to a more egalitarian setting arrangement is one practical means to achieve this end. Rather than "interviewing" the client, the process of taking a spiritual history should be seen as active, empathetic, participation in a one sided conversation

Table 1

Initial Narrative Framework

1. Describe the religious/spiritual tradition you grew up in. How did your family express its spiritual beliefs? How important was spirituality to your family? Extended family?

2. What sort of personal experiences (practices) stand out to you during your years at home? What made these experiences special? How have they informed your later life?

3. How have you transitioned or matured from those experiences? How would you describe your current spiritual/religious orientation? Is your spirituality a personal strength? If so, how?

Interpretive Anthropological Framework

1. Affect: What aspects of your spiritual life give you pleasure? What role does your spirituality play in handling life's sorrows? Enhancing its joys? Coping with its pain? How does your spirituality give you hope for the future? What do you wish to accomplish in the future?

2. Behavior: Are there particular spiritual rituals or practices that help you deal with life's obstacles? What is your level of involvement in faith-based or religious communities? How are they supportive? Are there spiritually encouraging individuals with whom you maintain contact?

3. Cognitive: What are your current religious/spiritual beliefs? What are they based upon? What beliefs do you find particularly meaningful? What does your faith say about trials? How does this belief help you overcome obstacles? How do your beliefs affect your health practices?

4. Communion: Describe your relationship with God. What has been your experience of God? How does the God communicate with you? How have these experiences encouraged you? Have

Table 1, Continued

there been times of deep spiritual intimacy? How does your relationship help you face life challenges? How would God describe you?

5. Conscience: How do you determine right and wrong? What are your key values? How does your spirituality help you deal with guilt (sin)? What role does forgiveness play in your life?

6. Intuition: To what extent do you experience intuitive hunches (flashes of creative insight, premonitions, spiritual insights)? Have these insights been a strength in your life? If so, how?

(Kisthardt, 1997). Accordingly, the practitioner's primary role is to listen attentively, and to help clients tell their stories while avoiding excessive interruption (Cowger, 1997). Empathetic and paraphrasing responses can be especially helpful in building rapport and cultivating an atmosphere in which clients feel comfortable sharing their spiritual experiences. The practitioner's aim should be to transmit acceptance and validation through physical and verbal language (Kisthardt, 1997). One pragmatic way to achieve this result is to use terminology that is congruent with the client's spiritual tradition, especially when they introduce such terms into the flow of conversation. For example, one might use the term *synagogue* when working with Jewish clients to refer to a Jewish house of worship. Similarly, one might use the term *imam*, a term for an Islamic religious leader, when working with Muslims.

Helping professionals assist clients in discovering, clarifying, and articulating their stories by employing a number of verbal following skills (Hepworth & Larsen, 1993). Minimal prompts ("And then what happened?" "And?" "But?"), accent responses (in which a key word or short phrase is repeated in a questioning tone of voice), and embedded questions ("I'm curious about . . . " "I'm interested in knowing . . .") all assist clients in relating their story without diverting attention away from the story itself.

While the spiritual history format described in the top half of Table 1 (above) provides a good understanding of clients' spirituality, it is The Interpretive Anthropological Framework delineated in the second half that provides a multidimensional framework for understanding the personal, subjective reality of spirituality in clients' lives. The questions contained in the Interpretive Framework are not necessarily provided for the purpose of having clients answer them in a sequential series. Rather, the intent is to alert practitioners to the various components of each domain, to create awareness concerning the potentiality of clients' spirituality.

Accordingly, within the context of clients' narratives, it is expected that practitioners will utilize certain questions, or adaptations, to flesh out clients' narratives at specific junctions using the methods discussed immediately above. For example, a practitioner might ask, using the tentative phrasing suggested previously, "I'm interested in knowing more about how your relationship with God has enabled you to face the challenges life has presented you with" when working with a Roman Catholic. Similarly, when working with a Native American from the Plains Ojibway, who gather to publicly confess their sins in the presence of Spirit, a practitioner might attempt to obtain further concreteness by asking how the ritual has assisted them in coping (Jacobs, 1992). In other words, the Interpretive Framework is to assist helping professionals in discovering and clarifying the spiritual strengths of clients as they relate their spiritual histories.

Overview of Common Spiritual Strengths

There are a number of empirically based spiritual strengths the Interpretive Anthropological Framework is designed to evoke. Although to some extent intertwined, the following is a list of common strengths that have some degree of empirical validation. Clearly, one's relationship with the Ultimate (Jesus for evangelical Christians, Jehovah for Jews, Allah for Muslims, God for Zoroastrians, sacred texts for Buddhists, Spirit for certain Native American tribes, etc.) is a key strength, facilitating coping, defeating loneliness, promoting a sense of mission and purpose, instilling a sense of personal worth and value, providing hope for the future, etc. (Ellison & Levin, 1998; Pargament, 1997; Perry, 1998).

Rituals, inherent in essentially every spiritual tradition, have been widely associated with positive outcomes and can serve to ease anxiety and dread, alleviate isolation, promote a sense of security, and establish a sense of being loved and appreciated (Ellison & Levin, 1998; Jacobs, 1992; Pargament, 1997; Perry, 1998; Worthington, Kurusu, McCullough & Sandage, 1996). Rituals commonly encountered in North American settings include: scripture reading, prayer, meditation, Holy Communion, ceremonial rites, Bar-Mitzvahs, rites of passage, baptisms, and confession of sins.

Participation in religious communities is also a significant strength (Calhoun-Brown, 1998; Cohen, Doyle, Skoner, Rabin & Gwaltney, 1997; Ellison & George, 1994; Ellison & Levin, 1998; Maton & Salem, 1995). This resource has been associated with elevated levels of empowerment, realization of personal strengths, coping ability, self-confidence, lovability, and sense of belonging. Common forms of participation include houses of worship (churches, synagogues, mosques, temples), small groups (Bible studies, Promise Keepers[2], prayer meetings, elder/mentoring gatherings, spirituality groups; tribal celebrations), and discipleship/mentoring dyads and triads.

The cognitive schemata associated with spiritual belief systems have also been widely documented as strengths (Ellison & Levin, 1998; Pargament, 1997; Perry, 1998; Worthington, et al., 1996). For example, knowing that one is loved unconditionally, that there is a deeper spiritual purpose to life which animates one's existence, can facilitate peacefulness, coping ability, etc.

There are other spiritual strengths the Interpretive Framework is also designed to elicit, such as intuition and methods for alleviating guilt. While these elements have received support in the practice literature as important resources (Krill, 1990), they have not been empirically validated as strengths, primarily due to a lack of research. However, it seems reasonable to suggest that having a framework for alleviating the occurrence of realistic guilt related to hurting another, violating an agreement, or transgressing one's value system, is a strength (Krill, 1990). Similarly, possessing an intuitive capability is easily seen as a strength. Anecdo-

---

[2] Promise Keepers is an evangelical Christian men's group. Further information on Promise Keepers can be found at their website, www.promisekeepers.org. Evangelical Christianity is often defined as a transdenominational, ecumenical movement that emphasizes the following historic Protestant tenets: (1) salvation only through personal trust in Christ's finished atoning work, (2) a spiritually transformed life marked by moral conduct and personal devotion such as scripture reading and missions, and (3) the Bible as authoritative and reliable (Marsden, 1987).

tal accounts indicate that creative hunches, flashes of insight, etc. are often a significant resource in clients' lives. Ultimately, it is the perceptions of clients that are central in determining their spiritual strengths. Regardless of previous empirical findings or anecdotal wisdom, it is clients who are the final arbitrators of their spiritual strengths. The purpose of the Interpretive Framework is merely to provide practitioners with a guide for eliciting commonly held spiritual strengths that may exist, and in the process, provide a smooth transition to the interventions the realized strengths suggest.

Interventions

Simply having clients articulate narratives that highlight their spiritual strengths is an effective intervention. As Laird (1994) notes, our stories help shape our evolving construction of reality, who we are, how we see the world, and our ability to lead successful lives. By having clients relate an area of prominent strength, an altered, therapeutically beneficial construction of reality is fostered. In turn, this new self-perception enables clients to ameliorate problems, by, for example, giving clients a new inner vocabulary which depicts them as capable individuals who have the resources and abilities to solve life's complex issues. As Saleebey (1997) notes, practitioners can assist clients in ameliorating their problems by providing a positive reflection of their capabilities, strengths, resiliency, and resources. This is effectively accomplished by using the Interpretive Framework to evoke a full array of clients' spiritual capabilities and resources.

The salutary effect achieved by this process can be facilitated by using diagrammatic instruments such as spiritual genograms to depict the flow of one's spiritual history over a number of generations. Another suggestion is to transpose the autobiographical material into a timeline in the form of a spiritual journey, or map, with pictorial representations of significant events and experiences. Both approaches effectively act as positive mirrors, reflecting clients' resilience and strengths.

Self psychology's concept of selfobjects and holding environments provides an additional mirroring intervention (Elson, 1986). As indicated in the previous section, in many cases God, and to certain extent religious communities, act as ideal selfobjects, a relationship that is readily revealed by the Interpretive Framework (How would God describe you? How does God feel about you?) Helping professionals can ameliorate problems by encouraging clients to enter into a nurturing holding environment with such selfobjects through increased prayer, meditation, and participation in religious communities. Such holding environments can foster increased ego cohesion, integration, and mastery (Elson, 1986). While this intervention may seem especially appropriate for those traditions that posit a caring Transcendent being (e.g., Christianity), its effectiveness has been demonstrated in atheistic traditions such as Buddhism (Emavardhana & Tori, 1997).

Cognitive and behavioral interventions, based upon clients' spiritual belief systems, have also been empirically validated. Replacing counterproductive beliefs and behaviors with productive ones drawn from the client's spiritual framework is often a salutary intervention (Propst, 1996). For example, with clients who believe that all events are imbued with spiritual meaning, (tapped by such questions as: "What does your faith say about trials?" "How does your spirituality help you overcome obstacles?"), a productive reframing can occur that shifts the focus away from the present obstacle to the spiritual lessons clients are desirous of learning (Saleebey, 1997). Overwhelmed by problems, clients can easily overlook the important spiritual development such trials foster, in spite of tradition specific injunctions which indicate that God is working all things together for a purpose. Similarly, prayer, meditation and spiritual mourning have all been used effectively as behaviorally based interventions (Worthington, et al., 1996).

Having clients access environmental resources represents an additional potential intervention (Sullivan, 1992). Typically, assessment reveals a number of environment strengths that can be utilized. Religious communities usually have programs, activities and social networks that can be beneficially used by clients to overcome obstacles and reorient their lives along ends more in keeping with their ultimate life goals.

Further, as Kisthardt (1997) suggests, assisting clients in their desire to grow spirituality can be an effective intervention. By focusing on areas of interest to clients, practitioners can facilitate personal growth and development that often result in reduction, and even amelioration, of impediments. As interest and competencies are extended in an area of interest, in this case some aspect of a client's desired spiritual aims, new competencies are often naturally leveraged to address other problem areas (Sullivan, 1997).

Cautions and Limitations

Spiritual assessment also engenders areas of concern. As O' Rourke (1997) has stated, practitioners must strike a delicate balance between using and, as noted directly above, developing clients' spiritual strengths on one hand, and remaining focused upon the present helping task on the other. The point of therapy should always remain on marshaling resources to ameliorate the presenting problem. Practitioners should avoid falling into the role of spiritual directors in which they assume the role of a spiritual expert directing clients in their spirituality, unless they are trained and sanctioned to provide these services.

Additionally, some practitioners may hold certain value positions so firmly that they risk imposing their positions on clients, in which case they should refrain from undertaking spiritual assessments with populations that are likely to hold differing values. Feminist practitioners strongly committed to an egalitarian family structure, for example, should engage in thorough self-examination before undertaking spiritual assessment with Muslim families, who commonly affirm complementary marriages. In such cases, the practitioner should consider referring the client to another therapist whose value system is more congruent with the client's.

Conclusion

As Hepworth and Larsen (1993, p. 192) note, "assessment is a critical process." As critical as assessment is for traditional practitioners, for those operating within the strengths perspective, assessment plays a role of even greater significance. Without proper assessment, strengths-based practitioners cannot fully develop an awareness of clients' assets, assets which are the central ethos of the perspective (Ronnau & Poertner, 1993).

By joining the narrative format of a spiritual history with an interpretive anthropological framework, this chapter has provided an assessment instrument that helps elicit the strengths resident in many clients. Accordingly, this chapter provides an assessment framework for operationalizing what may be the most untapped strength among clients: their spirituality.

References

Bergin, A. E., & Jensen, J. P. (1990). Religiosity of psychotherapists: A national survey. *Psychotherapy, 27*(1), 3-7.

Boyd, T. A. (1998). Spiritually sensitive assessment tools for social work practice. In B. Hugen (Ed.), *Christianity and social work: Readings on the integration of Christian faith and social work practice* (pp. 239-255). Botsford, CT: NACSW Press.

Bullis, R. K. (1996). *Spirituality in social work practice.* Washington, DC: Taylor & Francis.

Calhoun-Brown, A. (1998). While marching to Zion: Otherworldliness and racial empowerment in the black community. *Journal for the Scientific Study of Religion, 37*(3), 427-439.

Canda, E. R. (1997). Spirituality. In *1997 Supplement.* In R. L. Edwards (Ed.), *Encyclopedia of social work* (19, pp. 299-309). Washington, DC: NASW Press.

Carroll, M. M. (1997). Spirituality and clinical social work: Implications of past and current perspectives. *Arete, 62*(1), 25-34.

Cohen, S., Doyle, W. J., Skoner, D. P., Rabin, B. S., &

Gwaltney, J. M. J. (1997). Social ties and susceptibility to the common cold. *JAMA, 277*(24), 1940-1944.

Cornett, C. (1992). Toward a more comprehensive personology: Integrating a spiritual perspective into social work practice. *Social Work, 37*(2), 101-102.

Cowger, C. D. (1994). Assessing client strengths: Clinical assessments for client empowerment. *Social Work, 39*(3), 262-268.

Cowger, C. (1997). Assessing client strengths: Assessment for client empowerment. In D. Saleebey (Ed.), *The strengths perspective* (pp. 59-73). New York: Longman.

Cowley, A.-D. S. (1996). *Transpersonal social work treatment* (4, pp. 663-698). New York: The Free Press.

Derezotes, D. S. (1995). Spirituality and religiosity: Neglected factors in social work practice. *Arete, 20*(1), 1-15.

Dombeck, M., & Karl, J. (1987). Spiritual issues in mental health care. *Journal of Religion and Health, 26*(3), 183-197.

Ellison, C. G. (1993). Religious involvement and self-perception among Black Americans. *Social Forces, 71*(4), 1027-1055.

Ellison, C. G., & George, L., K. (1994). Religious involvement, social ties, and social support in a Southeastern community. *Journal for the Scientific Study of Religion, 33*(1), 46-61.

Ellison, C. G., & Levin, J. S. (1998). The religion-health connection: Evidence, theory, and future directions. *Health Education and Behavior, 25*(6), 700-720.

Elson, M. (1986). *Self psychology in clinical social work.* New York: W. W. Norton & Company.

Emavardhana, T., & Tori, C. D. (1997). Changes in self-concept, ego defense mechanisms, and religiosity following seven-day Vipassana meditation retreats. *Journal for the Scientific Study of Religion, 36*(2), 194-206.

Fitchett, G. (1993). *Assessing spiritual needs.* Minneapolis: Augsburg.

Fowler, J. W. (1981). Stages of faith: The psychology of human development and the quest for meaning. San Francisco: Harper & Row.

Franklin, C., & Jordan, C. (1995). Qualitative assessment: A methodological review. *Families in Society: The Journal of Contemporary Human Services, 76*(5), 281-295.

Furman, L. D., & Chandy, J. M. (1994). Religion and spirituality: A long-neglected cultural component of rural social work practice. *Human Services in the Rural Environment, 17*(3/4), 21-26.

Gallup, G. J., & Castelli, J. (1989). *The people's religion: American faith in the 90's.* New York: Macmillan Publishing.

Genia, V. (1990). Religious development: A synthesis and reformulation. *Journal of Religion and Health, 29*(2), 85-99.

George, L. K. (1997). Choosing among established assessment tools: Scientific demands and practical constraints. *Generations, 37*(1), 32-36.

Hartman, A. (1995). Diagrammatic assessment of family relationships. *Families in Society: The Journal of Contemporary Human Services, 76*(2), 111-122.

Hepworth, D. H., & Larsen, J. A. (1993). *Direct Social Work Practice* (4). Pacific Grove, CA: Brooks/Cole Publishing.

Hodge, D. R. (1998). Welfare reform and religious providers: An examination of the new paradigm. *Social Work & Christianity, 25*(3), 24-48.

Hoge, D. R. (1996). Religion in America: The demographics of belief and affiliation. In E. P. Shafranske (Ed.), *Religion and the clinical practice of psychology* (pp. 21-41). Washington, DC: American Psychological Association.

Hwang, S.-C., Cowger, C., D., & Saleebey, D. (1998). Utilizing strengths in assessment/another view: Is strengths-based practice becoming more common? *Families in Society: The Journal of Contemporary Human Services, 97*(1), 25-31.

Jacobs, C. (1997). Essay: On spirituality and social work practice. *Smith College of Studies in Social Work, 67*(2), 171-175.

Jacobs, J. L. (1992). Religious ritual and mental health. In J. Schumaker (Ed.), *Religion and mental health* (pp. 291-299). New York: Oxford University Press.

Kennedy, J. E., Davis, R. C., & Talyor, B. G. (1998). Changes in spirituality and well-being among victims of sexual assault. *Journal for the Scientific Study of Religion, 37*(2), 322-328.

Kilpatrick, A. C., & Holland, T. P. (1990). Spiritual dimensions of practice. *The Clinical Supervisor, 8*(2), 125-140.

Kisthardt, W. (1997). The strengths model of case management: Principles and helping functions. In D. Saleebey (Ed.), *The strengths perspective* (pp. 97-113). New York: Longman.

Krill, D. F. (1990). *Practice Wisdom*. Sage human services guides, vol. 62. London: Sage Publications.

Laird, J. (1994). "Thick description" revisited: Family therapist as anthropologist-constructivist. In E. Sherman & W. J. Reid (Eds.), *Qualitative research in social work* (pp. 175-189). New York: Columbia University Press.

Lovinger, R. J. (1996). Considering the religious dimension in assessment and treatment. In E. Shafranske (Ed.), *Religion and the clinical practice of psychology* (pp. 327-364). Washington, DC: American Psychological Association.

Lukoff, D., Turner, R., & Lu, F. (1993). Transpersonal psychology research review: Psychospiritual dimensions of healing. *The Journal of Transpersonal Psychology, 25*(1), 11-28.

Marsden, G. M. (1991). *Understanding fundamentalism and evangelicalism.* Grand Rapids: Eerdmans Publishing.

Maton, K. I., & Salem, D. A. (1995). Organizational characteristics of empowering community settings: A multiple case study approach. *American Journal of Community Practice, 23*(5), 631-656.

Mattaini, M. A., & Kirk, S. A. (1993). Points & viewpoints: Misdiagnosing assessment. *Social Work, 38*(2), 231-233.

Mattaini, M. A., & Kirk, S. A. (1991). Assessing assessment in social work. *Social Work, 36*(3), 260-266.

Montgomery, C. (1994). Swimming upstream: The strengths of women who survive homelessness. *Advanced Nursing Science, 16*(3), 34-45.

Muffler, J., Langrod, J. G., & Larson, D. (1992). "There is a balm in Gilead": Religion and substance abuse treatment. In J. H. Lowinson, P. Ruiz & R. B. Millman (Eds.), *Substance Abuse: A comprehensive textbook* (2). Baltimore: Williams & Wilkins (584-595).

Nathanson, I., G. (1995). Divorce and women's spirituality. *Journal of Divorce and Remarriage, 22*(3/4), 179-188.

Nee, W. (1968). *The spiritual man* (Vol. 1-3). New York: C F P.

Nino, A. G. (1997). Assessment of spiritual quests in clinical practice. *International Journal of Psychotherapy, 2*(2), 192-212.

O' Rourke, C. (1997). Listening for the sacred: Addressing spiritual issues in the group treatment of adults with mental illness. *Smith College of Studies in Social Work, 67*(2), 179-196.

Pargament, K. I. (1997). *The psychology of religion and coping.* New York: Guilford Press.

Peck, M. S. (1993). *Further along the road less traveled.* New York: Simon & Schuster.

Perry, B. G. F. (1998). The relationship between faith and well-being. *Journal of Religion and Health, 37*(2), 125-136.

Poole, D. L. (1998). Politically correct or culturally competent? *Health and Social Work, 23*(3), 163-166.

Propst, L. R. (1996). Cognitive-behavioral therapy and the religious person. In E. P. Shafranske (Ed.), *Religion and the clinical practice of psychology* (pp. 391-407). Washington, DC: American Psychological Association.

Pruyser, P. (1976). *The minister as diagnostician.* Philadelphia: Westminister Press.

Rauch, J. B. (1993). *Assessment: A sourcebook for social work practice.* Milwaukee: Families International.

Reed, P. G. (1992). An emerging paradigm for the investigation of spirituality in nursing. *Research in Nursing and Health, 15,* 349-357.

Rey, L. D. (1997). Religion as invisible culture: Knowing about and knowing with. *Journal of Family Social Work, 2*(2), 159-177.

Rizzuto, A.-M. (1996). Psychoanalytic treatment and the religious person. In E. Shafranske (Ed.), *Religion and the clinical practice of psychology* (pp. 409-431). Washington, DC: American Psychological Association.

Robbins, S. P., Chatterjee, P., & Canda, E. R. (1998). *Contemporary human behavior theory.* Boston: Allyn & Bacon.

Rodman, M. K. (1987). Naturalistic inquiry: An alternative model for social work assessment. *Social Services Review, 61*(2), 231-246.

Ronnau, J., & Poertner, J. (1993). Identification and use of strengths: A family system approach. *Children Today, 22*(2), 20-23.

Saleebey, D. (1992). Introduction: Power to the people. In D. Saleebey (Ed.), *The strengths perspective* (pp. 3-17). New York: Longman.

Saleebey, D. (1997). The strengths approach to practice. In D. Saleebey (Ed.), *The strengths perspective* (pp. 49-57). New York: Longman.

Scott, D. (1989). Meaning construction in social work practice. *Social Services Review, 63,* 39-51.

Sermabeikian, P. (1994). Our clients, ourselves: The spiritual perspective and social work practice. *Social Work, 39*(2), 178-183.

Sheridan, M. J., Bullis, R. K., Adcock, C. R., Berlin, S. D., & Miller, P. C. (1992). Practitioners' personal and professional attitudes and behaviors toward religion and spirituality: Issues for education and practice. *Journal of Social Work Education, 28*(2), 190-203.

Sherwood, D. A. (1998). Spiritual assessment as a normal part of social work practice: Power to help and power to harm. *Social Work & Christianity, 25*(2), 80-100.

Spero, M. H. (1990). Parallel dimensions of experience in psychoanalytic psychotherapy of the religious patient. *Psychotherapy, 27*(1), 53-71.

Sperry, L., & Giblin, P. (1996). Marital and family therapy with religious persons. In E. Shafranske (Ed.), *Religion and the clinical practice of psychology* (pp. 511-532). Washington, DC: American Psychological Association.

Strickland, L. (1994). Autobiographical interviewing and narrative analysis: An approach to psychosocial assessment. *Clinical Social Work Journal, 22*(1), 27-41.

Sullivan, W. P. (1992). Reconsidering the environment as a helping resource. In D. Saleebey (Ed.), *The strengths perspective* (pp. 148-157). White Plains, NY: Longman.

Sullivan, W. P. (1997). On strengths, niches, and recovery from serious mental illness. In D. Saleebey (Ed.), *The strengths perspective* (pp. 183-199). New York: Longman.

Tan, S.-Y. (1996). Religion in clinical practice: Implicit and explicit integration. In E. Shafranske (Ed.), *Religion and the clinical practice of psychology* (pp. 365-387). Washington, DC: American Psychological Association.

Ventis, W. L. (1995). The relationship between religion and mental health. *Journal of Social Issues, 51*(2), 33-48.

Worthington, E. J., Kurusu, T., McCullough, M., & Sandage, S. (1996). Empirical research on religion and psychotherapeutic processes and outcomes: A 10-year review and research prospectus. *Psychological Bulletin, 119*(3), 448-487.

CHAPTER THREE

Spiritual Lifemaps: A Client-Centered Pictorial Instrument for Spiritual Assessment, Planning, and Intervention[3]

This chapter develops and orients practitioners to, a new pictorial instrument for spiritual assessment--the spiritual lifemap. After introducing the concept of spiritual lifemaps, I suggest how to construct a lifemap, conduct an assessment, and use the instrument to elicit spiritually-based interventions. A number of common interventions are delineated, including the use of the instrument itself as an intervention. The chapter concludes with a brief discussion of other settings in which lifemaps can be used and possible value conflicts that may arise when assessing spirituality.

Spiritual lifemaps: Philosophy and advantages

The philosophical roots of the instrument can be traced back through 16 centuries of Christian spiritual direction tradition to the African writer Augustine (354-430/1991) and his seminal work, the Confessions, which is widely considered to be the first autobiographical work in recorded human history (Clark, 1993). In what Clark (1993, p. 39) refers to as "an act of therapy," this biography chronicles Augustine's spiritual journey.

Similarly, spiritual lifemaps are a pictorial delineation of clients' spiritual journey. At its most basic level, a drawing pencil is used to sketch various spiritually significant life events on paper. Thus, much like road maps, spiritual lifemaps tell us where we have come from, where we are now, and where we are going. The method is analogous to various approaches drawn from art and family therapy in which a client's history is depicted on a "lifeline" (Tracz & Gehart-Brooks, 1999). However, as in the Confes-

---

[3] Much of the material in this chapter will be appearing in an upcoming issue of *Social Work* in an article written by D. R. Hodge entitled, "Spiritual lifemaps: A client-centered pictorial instrument for spiritual assessment, planning, and intervention" (in press). This material is used in this book with the permission of NASW.

sions, the narrative is based upon the client's spiritual pilgrimage and associated events. Put simply, a spiritual lifemap is an illustrated account of the client's relationship with God over time--a map of his or her spiritual life.

Building upon the strengths of the constructivist perspective, spiritual lifemaps offer users a number of advantages. By placing a client-constructed medium at the center of assessment, clients are involved in the therapeutic process in a significant way, essentially from the beginning of therapy. Through the creation of a lifemap, the message is implicitly communicated that the client is a pro-active, self-directed, fully engaged participant in the therapeutic process.

Possible resistance and anxiety may also be ameliorated through the use of a non-verbal, pictorially-based medium. Given the highly personal nature of spirituality for many clients, and many practitioners' limited training regarding various spiritual cosmologies (Canda & Furman, 1999), practitioners may inadvertently offend clients, jeopardizing the therapeutic relationship, when using verbally-based spiritual assessment approaches. The pictorial instrument affords practitioners the opportunity to focus on building therapeutic rapport by providing an atmosphere that is accepting, nonjudgmental, and supportive during the initial assessment (Kahn, 1999). Additionally, individuals who are not verbally oriented may find pictorial expression more conducive to their personal communication styles (McNiff, 1992). Further, clients may find it less threatening having a concrete object which functions as the focus of subsequent conversation rather than the client (Moon, 1994).

Finally, given the amorphous, subjective nature of spirituality, physical depiction may help concretize clients' extant strengths (Hodge, 2000a). In other words, the process of conceptualizing and depicting one's spiritual journey may help to focus and objectify spiritual assets, which can then be discussed and marshaled to address problems.

Broaching the topic of spirituality with clients

Since many clients desire to incorporate their spirituality into therapeutic concerns, clients often spontaneously mention spiritual resources (e.g., God, church, prayer, etc.) during initial sessions. Practitioners can acknowledge and validate these statements and briefly explore the salience of spirituality in the client's life (e.g., "How important is spirituality or religion to you?"). If it appears that a spiritual assessment might be appropriate, the practitioner should explain the basic concept of a lifemap to the client, highlighting how it might be used to operationalize spiritual strengths to overcome presenting difficulties.

Alternatively, practitioners can ask at the start of therapy, or at a later junction, if spirituality/religion serves as a resource in the client's life. Upon an affirmative response, the instrument can be explained. In either case, it is important to procure clients' consent before proceeding with a spiritual assessment and the actual drawing of the lifemap (Doherty, 1999).

Conducting an Assessment with Lifemaps

In keeping with evidence that suggests information is stored and organized narratively in the mind (Strickland, 1994), events are usually depicted chronologically, from birth through to the present, and usually continuing on to death and the client's transition to the afterlife. More specifically, a path, a roadway, or a single line is commonly used to represent the spiritual sojourn. One way to proceed is to draw this path on the paper first, break the path into years or decades, and then fill in events along the path, a method that ensures that equal space is allotted to all points along the lifecycle. Conversely, others might prefer a more freeform approach in which one's path and life events are sketched together. Among the advantages of this approach, is the opportunity to devote more space to significant time periods during one's spiritual walk.

Symbols drawn from the client's spiritual cosmology are typically used to mark key events along the journey. For instance, a cross might be used by a Christian to portray a spiritual conversion, while a depiction of the Lingam and Yoni might be used by a Hindu to represent her relationship to Siva. Similarly, a stick figure in a meditative pose enveloped in a sunbeam might signify a time of enlightenment for a New Age adherent.

Concurrently, since most spiritual cosmologies conceive material existence to be an extension of the sacred reality (Richards & Bergin, 1997), important "secular" incidents are usually included. Both positive (marriage, the birth of a child) and particularly negative events (death, loss of a job, and other trials) may be portrayed. The ultimate goal is the depiction of all events that are perceived to be of spiritual significance by the client on the lifemap.

To fully operationalize the potential of the instrument, it is important to ask clients to highlight the various trials they have encountered and the spiritual resources they have used to cope in the course of their journeys. As noted above, symbolic depictions can be effectively employed. Hills, bumps and potholes, rain, clouds, lightning, etc. might be used to portray difficult stations along the spiritual sojourn, for instance, while various symbols might also be developed to represent spiritual assets that have facilitated coping. Finally, while providing general guidelines and, if necessary, specific tips for the construction of lifemaps, client creativity and self-expression should be encouraged.

To assist clients in the creative expression of their spiritual journeys, it is important to have a good supply of various media readily available (Horovitz-Darby, 1994). Drawing instruments might include drawing pencils (specifically No. 1) and erasers (Mars Staetler and gum), colored drawing pencils (a 12 color set), fine and broad nibbed colored markers (an 8 color set) and large and small crayons (at least 16 colors). It is also helpful to provide a choice of white and manila paper (sizes 8.5" x 11" to 24" x 36"), as well as colored construction paper (sizes 8.5" x 11" and 12" x 18"). Practitioners may also wish to make available scissors, glue sticks, and rulers as well as a variety of magazines and newspapers. Clients may wish to clip items from the latter media (e.g., "AUTO ACCIDENT") and paste them onto the lifemap to illustrate specific events that hold meaningful places in their spiritual walk. Due to the amount of data lifemaps elicit, it is usually best to use a large sheet of paper on which to sketch the map.

Some clients, when faced with a large blank sheet of paper, may experience "stage fright" and have difficulty beginning or, later on in the process, may feel inadequate to express a certain event or concept. In such cases, it is generally appropriate to encourage individuals to plunge ahead and draw (McNiff, 1992), noting that there is no correct way to draw a lifemap. It may also help to stress that the central function of lifemaps is to express and communicate a spiritual reality rather than to assess someone's artistic talent (Kahn, 1999). A drawing using stick figures is just as valid as one with more elaborate portrayals.

As implied in the preceding section, during the creation of a lifemap, practitioners adopt a secondary, supportive role, assisting and encouraging the client as needed. The goal is to help clients tell their stories while nurturing an affirming, empathetic relationship. For example, practitioners might offer to clip out material from magazines if clients elect to use such media.

Upon the completion of the lifemap, the practitioner should generally ask the client to explain their creation ("Would you tell me about your spiritual lifemap?"). As clients express their spiritual journeys, it is critical that practitioners demonstrate interest, curiosity, and even fascination with their clients' narratives (Bullis, 1996). Minimal verbal prompts ("But?" "And?" "Yes"), accent responses (in which a word or short phrase is repeated in a questioning tone), in conjunction with typical emphatic responses should be used during this stage of the assessment (Hepworth & Larsen, 1993). Practitioners should attempt to place their own beliefs on the shelf and seek to understand clients' phenomenological spiritual reality.

Helping professionals should be aware that many clients may be hesitant to trust practitioners due to concerns that practitioners will not treat with honor that which they hold to be sacred (Furman, Perry & Goldale, 1996). To a great extent, the practitioner can alleviate this apprehension by expressing genuine emphatic support. Further, respecting clients' spiritual reality as an equally valid construction of reality on a par with the dominant secular framework helps to foster an environment in which spiritual interventions can be more productively explored (Bullis, 1996).

A Case Example

Diagram 1 (see pg. 39) indicates what a completed lifemap might look like on a smaller scale. The client, a 42-year-old Black male referred to as Darrin, grew up as an only child in a two-parent middle class home. His formative years were characterized by heavy involvement in sports and warm, caring relationships. However, upon leaving home at 18, it was as if he entered a different, more tumultuous, reality. Seemingly aimless wondering, a stormy dating relationship, and an inability to break out of repetitive, often-unhealthy patterns marked his life during his early to mid-20s. After breaking off the dating relationship he experienced a series of forks, wrong turns, and dead ends, which led him to cry out to God in desperation. His life continued to spiral out of control until he ended up at the foot of the cross "DOA," figuratively dead on arrival.

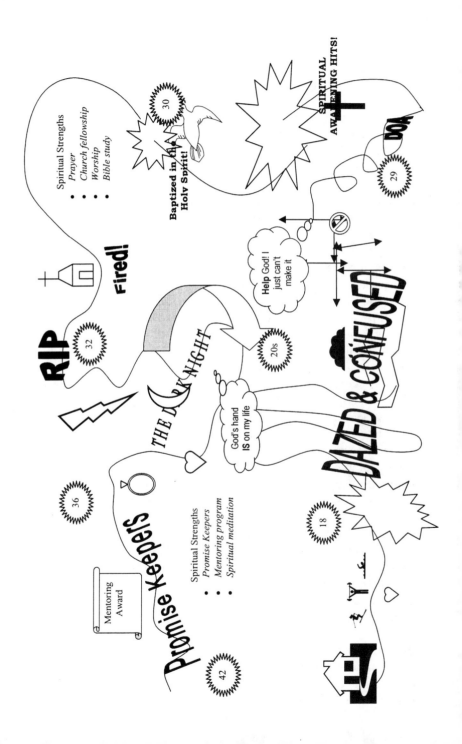

At 29, Darrin experienced a spiritual awakening that resulted in him entering another reality. This experience marked a sharp turning point in his life. A year later he joined a Pentecostal church, and experienced a new infilling of the Holy Spirit, symbolized by a dove on his lifeline, which opened an additional dimension of the spiritual world. In addition to his relationship with Jesus, he lists his spiritual strengths as prayer, church fellowship, worship, and Bible study.

Although being fired from his job was a difficult experience, his church fellowship played an instrumental role in helping him through the situation. More difficult to deal with was the sudden death of his parents at age 32, which hit him like an emotional lightening bolt. Over the next few years, other difficulties emerged, such as friction with some church members, close friends moving away, and fewer spiritually vibrant times of prayer and Bible study. Eventually, the sense of God's presence slowly left him. As he reached the point of questioning his relationship with God, his existence, and the validity of his own life, Darrin experienced a series of events that served to alter the course of his life. Through these events, which he saw as providential, he realized that God had not abandoned him. Soon after that, his "dark night" of the soul ended as he fully realized God's love for him.

At 36, Darrin married a woman from his church. A couple of years later, he was presented with a mentoring award on behalf of his efforts with troubled youth. Although he finds the relationships draining at times, his friendships with the other men and the youth are also invigorating. Similarly, he also draws strength from the male intimacy he finds in his Promise Keepers small group, which he joined about the same time. He enjoys the opportunity the group provides for black men to share their experiences with racism with a receptive audience of whites, in addition to the encouragement he receives to be a better husband. Finally, in addition to these and the resources mentioned above, Darrin has recently found a significant source of spiritual strength meditating on meaningful Bible verses.

Planning Interventions

As the above condensed narrative implies, spiritual lifemaps are designed to unfold clients' orienting framework to practitioners. Spiritual cosmologies, like all orienting systems, provide adherents with a general framework for interpreting the world. Similarly, during times of stress, situations in which individuals are more likely to encounter helping professionals, these frameworks help clients understand the challenges they face. As a result, it is important that practitioners have some understanding of these frameworks so that they are aware of how clients approach the difficulties they encounter.

Further, during acute trials, these frameworks for understanding reality frequently become more salient (Pargament, 1997). Put differently, problems often serve to re-orient individuals towards their metaphysical reality and increase its level of personal importance for adherents—the "no atheists in foxholes" effect. Consequently, spiritually based coping provides individuals with an added resource to address difficulties (Pargament, 1997). However, it is also true that clients can become so mired in present, often chronic challenges that they overlook potential resources that may solve current obstacles (Saleebey, 1997), hence the need for assessment and intervention that can then use those spiritual strengths.

Thus, when considering interventions based upon clients' spiritual lifemaps, two questions are of particular interest to practitioners. First, how have clients culled various resources from their frameworks during past difficulties to ameliorate problems? Second, what types of unaccessed resources are available in this framework that can be marshaled to address current problems?

In practice settings, this means that therapists make a smooth transition from general inquiry to exploring how clients have dealt with past trials as well as the strengths that exist in the client's spirituality. Thus, practitioners should ask clients to elaborate on the various trials they have delineated on their lifemaps as well as seek to identify various assets that can be used to address current obstacles. In the above case example, a practitioner might wish to explore in more detail how Darrin's spiritual strengths helped him to deal with past trials and how they might be used to address his present difficulties. How questions (How did you cope with that event?) and embedded questions (I'm interested in knowing more about what you consider to be your spiritual strengths?) can often be effectively used to elicit further information.

Hodge (2000b) has delineated a number of pathways through which spirituality may engender positive outcomes. Paraphrased pathways that are of particular importance are one's relationship to God (or the perceived Transcendent), spiritual beliefs, spiritual rituals or practices, and the support of a religious community. These pathways, which are empirically based and found in most religious traditions, provide guidance for eliciting specific spiritual strengths. Table 2 (see pg. 43) provides a list of common questions that might be asked to help operationalize clients' spiritual assets in these areas.

The questions delineated in Table 2 are not meant to be asked in any specific order, nor should practitioners necessarily retain their exact wording. Rather, practitioners should be familiar with the questions and interlace them with clients' lifemaps in the natural flow of conversation. It is probable that clients will depict a number of the four pathways on their lifemaps in some form. The questions should be adapted to facilitate the exploration of key events and themes with the lifemap serving as the focal point around which the discussion is based.

In instances where some of the four pathways do not appear on the lifemap, or in subsequent discussion, practitioners should consider inquiring regarding their salience. As mentioned above, these pathways are found in most traditions. Thus, it is likely that they have played some role in clients' spiritual journey. In such cases, tentative praising should be used (I was wondering if there are particular rituals that have nurtured your spirituality in some instances during your spiritual journey?). In light of subsequent inquiry, clients may wish to adapt their lifemap.

Finally, when asking questions, and in general when interacting with clients, practitioners should allow clients to fill in their terminology. For example, although the questions delineated in Table 2 (see pg. 43) use the term "God" in keeping with the beliefs of most clients in United States (Gallup & Castelli, 1989), this and other terminology should be adapted to the reflect the terms of the client's spiritual cosmology. For example, one would not use the term "God" when working with Buddhist traditions that do not believe in God as an expression of the Transcendent. As discussed in the previous chapter, during assessment practitioners should attempt to understand clients' spiritual cosmologies and then incorporate the resulting terms and concepts into subsequent discussion.

Table 2

Possible Exploratory Questions for Clarifying Spiritual Assets

Relationship with God

"How did your relationship with God help you to address that problem?" "What did God teach you about that situation?" "Have you been able to apply those lessons in other situations?" "How has God supported you in times of crisis?" "What are the spiritual strengths of your relationship with God?" "How does God view you/feel about you?"

Spiritual Beliefs

"What does your faith teach about trials?" "Are there spiritual reasons for life's challenges?" "What are your favorite scriptures?" "Are there certain scriptures that really speak to you during times of stress?" "What spiritual principles have you learned from life's experiences?"

Spiritual Rituals

"Are there certain rituals or regular spiritual practices that help you cope with life's trials?" "Are some rituals particularly effective in certain situations?" "Are there particular rituals that strengthen your relationship with God?"

Religious Social Support

"What role has your church or religious community played during the crisis? "Are there relationships in your church that are particularly supportive?" "Has there been a spiritual mentor in your life that has been particularly significant?" "How have these individuals assisted you in coping with trials?"

Possible Interventions

To a large degree, the interventions that are mutually decided upon will depend upon the clients' spirituality and the theoretical orientation of the practitioner. There are, however, a number of possible interventions of which practitioners should be cognizant.

The following are examples of interventions that may be derived from spiritual lifemaps.

1. Spiritual Holding Environment

For practitioners familiar with self psychology, this theoretical framework, with its concept of selfobjects and holding environments offers what could be considered the ideal mirroring intervention (Elson, 1986). In many spiritual traditions, God can be understood as the ideal self-object, a caring, loving, benevolent, and compassionate Being. As implied above within the Christian framework, for instance, God is held to have so deeply loved individuals that the life of his Son was sacrificed on their behalf.

If assessment indicates that such a view of God is held, problems can be ameliorated by encouraging clients to enter into a nurturing holding environment through increased prayer and meditation on God's traits that are similar to those of ideal selfobjects. Such holding environments can foster increased ego cohesion, integration, and mastery (Elson, 1986) and may be particularly effective with disadvantaged populations, such as African-Americans, who often experience relatively fewer positive affirmations in the wider culture (Ellison, 1993).

2. Spiritual reframing

Spiritual reframing can be a powerful intervention. As suggested above, in the midst of present material difficulties, clients often forget the superseding metaphysical reality. In a forest of troubles, clients can lose sight of the spiritual truth that gives them hope, meaning and helps them endure trials and persevere through hardship.

As Pargament (1997) has noted, practitioners can assist clients by reframing their current situation in a manner that accents the spiritual reality. By altering the meanings clients attach to events, the significance of the event is changed. A situation that once seemed unfathomable and unbearable, by changing the attributions, can be endured, explained, and even become a valuable experience.

Spiritual lifemaps and subsequent exploration can be used to identify spiritual beliefs that help clients re-envision their current circumstances through a spiritual lens. Indeed, as illustrated above, this belief is often implicitly highlighted by spiritual lifemaps. During Darrin's "dark night of the soul" period, his realization that God had a plan for his life and had allowed the difficult events he experienced to touch his life for an underlying purpose dramatically altered his perceptions. While it is important to acknowledge the affective component of the present troublesome event, by reframing it as an opportunity for spiritual growth, a more hopeful outlook can be fostered (Pargament, 1997).

3. Cognitive reframing

A related intervention is cognitive reframing. In this approach, unhealthy beliefs are identified in keeping with the tenets of standard cognitive therapy. Helpful beliefs drawn from the individual's spiritual cosmology are then substituted for the deleterious beliefs.

For example, with Muslims, after the unproductive beliefs have been identified, they may be modified or replaced with beliefs derived from the Quran. This approach has been demonstrated to be at least as effective as traditional forms of therapy with Muslims for anxiety disorders (Azhar, Varma & Dharap, 1994), bereavement (Azhar & Varma, 1995a), and depression (Azhar & Varma, 1995b), while ameliorating problems at a faster rate in all three studies. Similarly positive outcomes have been found with Christians in addressing depression (Hawkins, Tan & Turk, 1999; Propst, 1996) and devout Mormons in addressing perfectionism (Richards, Owen & Stein, 1993).

4. Solution-focused rituals

Rituals that are spiritual strengths can be interfaced with solution-focused approaches to address problems. For example, in the above case example, exceptions to problems (e.g., the temptation to abuse alcohol when angry with his wife) may occur after participation in a particular church function, devotional activity, or Promise Keepers meeting. Participation in these events can then be substituted for the problem-causing activity, facilitating the adoption of more beneficial patterns of interaction (Hodge, 2000a).

Additionally, many rituals have been associated with positive mental health outcomes (Ellison & Levin, 1998; McCullough & Larson, 1999; Pargament, 1997; Worthington, Kurusu, McCullough & Sandage, 1996). For example, Jacobs (1992) notes that the regular gathering of the Plains Ojibway to confess their sins publicly fosters lower levels of anxiety and greater social bonding. Accordingly, enhancing the significance of rituals in clients' lives may foster positive ripple effects. Thus, independent of any existing therapeutic approach, the adoption of rituals can be considered an intervention.

5. Leveraging church-based social support

The social support obtained in religious settings is often both qualitatively and quantitatively superior that that found in other settings, and may be particularly efficacious among disadvantaged populations that often have fewer resources to draw upon (Ellison & George, 1994; Haight, 1998; Perry, 1998). Churches and allied organizations frequently provide a network of unique services and programs to assist individuals. For instance, Nason-Clark (1998) found that evangelical Christian groups offered a level of healing and support for female survivors of family violence that secular care providers were unable to match.

Practitioners can help clients explore the various options that may exist in this area. In addition to exploring current resources, Lifemaps may reveal assets that clients had not accessed due to the overwhelming nature of the current situation. It may also be possible to leverage existing or past assets to address current problems. For example, within the context of the case example, a practitioner might explore the possibility of leveraging church resources which were so effective in assisting Darrin to cope with his employment loss, to address present difficulties.

6. Brevity of life reflection

Spiritual lifemaps are also well suited for interventions in existential therapeutic approaches that focus on the brevity of life. By promoting a realistic appraisal of the brevity of life, the available opportunities, and the identification of achievable goals, significant change can be fostered. Similarly, by guiding clients into a positive confrontation with death, a new appreciation for life and an awareness of the preciousness of present and future time can be engendered, which in turn assists clients in accepting the challenge of solving present problems, setting new goals, and deciding to experience life in all its tumultuous fullness (Ellerman, 1999).

It is important to note that caution should be exercised when using brevity of life interventions. Practitioners should ensure that clients' affective state is compatible with such interventions. This being said, lifemaps are ideally suited for existential interventions as they intrinsically highlight the transitory nature of life and the inevitability of death, especially in systematic portrayals of the full lifecycle. As was illustrated in the case example, in freeform maps, clients may neglect to depict their future. Practitioners can transition into this area by highlighting the proportion of life lived as compared to the client's remaining time given current life expectancy rates. Similarly, heightening awareness of death and impending accountability in the afterlife, a view held by most of the population as well as most spiritual traditions (Gallup & Castelli, 1989), can increase motivation to change existing patterns.

Practitioners may also be able to foster an increased willingness to accept the existential anxiety of life, a greater willingness to accept life's experiences, both positive and negative, by focusing on the providential care of God. As in the case example, in many instances lifemaps will reveal that clients believe that life is lived under the care of God and that nothing happens to them apart from God's will. Belief in this reality can provide an added incentive to abandon oneself to the fullness of life.

Lifemaps as an Intervention

It is also important to note that the process of creating a spiritual lifemap, in addition to delineating material that can be used for planning interventions, is itself an intervention. As mentioned above, Augustine's Confessions, the animating concept of lifemaps, can be understood as "an act of therapy" (Clark, 1993, p. 39). Hence the concept's widespread use in spiritual direction, an approach that shares many similarities with psychotherapy (Ganje-Fling & McCarthy, 1991). Accordingly, listed below are a number of therapeutically beneficial traits that lifemaps may engender.

Being asked to create, to visually depict a spiritual lifemap, may promote self-esteem and enhance self-image (Burke, 1985). By requesting that the client construct an important therapeutic module, the message is sent that the client is capable, important, and has a significant role to play. It is empowering in the sense that it implicitly calls clients to take responsibility for their personal growth by taking an active part in the therapeutic process. Additionally, completing the construction of a lifemap sets in place a pattern of successfully tackling and completing tasks from the beginning of therapy.

The depiction of life events can foster significant reappraisal of previous events that had been evaluated in a negative light.

Physically illustrating situations can help reframe unconscious attributions that shape current actions (Weishaar, 1999). For instance, Darrin may have internalized parental messages believing he was a failure for "wasting" his youth and not obtaining a college degree. Yet after viewing his spiritual walk he may change his perceptions and see himself as a successful individual who has achieved a number of accomplishments (e.g., leadership roles in church activities, the mentoring program, Promise Keepers' groups, etc.).

Further, viewing past events through the lens of one's spiritual journey can help engender hope for the future. For example, reflecting on past failures as part of God's plan often enables individuals to discern the Divine's underlying reason for allowing the "failures" to occur. Upon reviewing his sojourn, Darrin may realize his "dazed and confused" period was instrumental to his later work in the mentoring program, allowing him to form stronger bonds with youths. Knowing that past difficult events had a discernible purpose gives clients confidence that current events also have a reason, which frequently reduces the perceived size of the present difficulty as well as fostering motivation to address the present situation.

Similarly, spiritual lifemaps can help shrink clients' existential vacuum. Emotional symptoms and problems can flourish when clients feel that meaning and purpose are absent (Lantz, 1998). Helping the client remember, recover, and become fully aware of past meaningful events reduces the sense of meaninglessness. Lifemaps, take a subjective, mysterious, elusive reality that may even be inaccessible through traditional verbal forms of communication and transforms it into a concrete observable depiction. In doing so, it helps recover meanings that may have been obscured (Moon, 1994). Further, specifically focusing on the spiritual nature of life is likely to increase perceptions of purpose and meaning (Pargament, 1997).

Lifemaps can also help free clients from the dominant discourses that restrict their choices (Richert, 1999). By depicting an alternative, strengths-based spiritual discourse, a new reality is fostered which, in turn, allows for new options to be discovered. As clients chart their spiritual narratives, old constraining stories can seem less attractive and may be discarded for the new empowering stories they are depicting.

Finally, it should be noted that practitioners can enhance the intrinsic benefits of lifemaps through specific interventions. For example, with the above case study, practitioners might heighten the sense of meaning and coherence in Darrin's life by asking if his "dazed and confused" period is now being used by God in his mentoring ministry. Indeed, many of the interventions delineated in the previous section dovetail with the material presented in this section. In short, practitioners are encouraged to incorporate interventions from their own theoretical orientations that are congruent with the strengths of the instrument to enhance its effectiveness as an intervention.

Other Applications

There are a number of other applications that should be briefly mentioned. In situations where conserving therapeutic time is crucial, some practitioners may wish to assign the creation of a lifemap as a homework assignment. The completed lifemap could then be discussed in the next therapeutic session. Alternatively, some practitioners may wish to perform their initial spiritual assessment with a spiritual ecomap (Hodge, 2000a), which may offer a faster assessment approach, and use the lifemap as a later intervention in the form of a homework assignment.

An important tenet in solution-focused therapeutic modalities is to reinforce positive changes that occur (Kok & Leskela, 1996). Lifemaps can be used to track these changes. For instance, the current section of the spiritual journey can be blown up off to one side, like voice captions in cartoons, so that the present therapeutic endeavor can be sketched in greater detail. Proposed interventions can be drawn on the lifemap along with their completion. Used in this way, lifemaps can serve as pictorial chronology of the therapeutic process.

Consequently, in the termination phase of therapy, lifemaps can then be used to conclude the sessions on a positive note by documenting the changes that have occurred during therapy. Further, they can be used for relapse prevention. Clients could, for example, be asked to periodically review their lifemaps to reinforce the gains they have made during counseling.

Value Conflicts

When discussing spirituality, it is imperative that clients' autonomy be respected (Cornett, 1992). Practitioners should carefully monitor their own and their client's responses to ensure that self-determination is preserved. Practitioners must be particularly sensitive when working with clients from different spiritual traditions that may evoke religious countertransference issues for the practitioner.

For instance, 44% of Sheridan and associates' (1992) sample of clinical social workers (N = 109) no longer participate in the religious affiliation of their childhood, with the change in religious affiliation occurring predominantly in a shift from Christianity, to none or "other." Additionally, more than one in three (36%) of these social workers reported ambivalent to negative feelings towards their religious backgrounds (Sheridan, et al., 1992). Since social work education is unlikely to have addressed the need to work through these negative feelings before interacting with Christians (Canda & Furman, 1999), these workers may be susceptible to religious countertransference biases that may imperil the therapeutic relationship (Dor-Shav, Friedman & Tcherbonogura, 1978). Additionally gay, lesbian and feminist practitioners who believe that mainstream Christian values are morally wrong should consider their ability to work with this population in a constructive fashion, as should the latter population when the seating at the therapeutic table is reversed.

Concern is also warranted when the value systems of practitioner and client are similar (Dor-Shav, et al., 1978). As noted above, the philosophy animating the lifemap is derived from the spiritual direction tradition, hence the instrument's ability to foster a large amount of clinically salient spiritual data. Yet, while there is a high degree of congruency between therapy and spiritual direction (Ganje-Fling & McCarthy, 1991), it is important to remain focused on solving clients' problems and to avoid falling into spiritual direction, in which the goal is to assist individuals to deepen their intimacy with God rather than to ameliorate problems. This temptation may be particularly prominent when the practitioner and the client are from the same spiritual tradition and the practitioner has an interest in spirituality.

Conclusion

Spiritual lifemaps offer practitioners a number of ways to integrate clients' spirituality into the therapeutic dialogue. Lifemaps can be used as an assessment tool, to plan spiritually based interventions, and they can stand alone as an intervention. They may be used in clinical settings or assigned as homework. They provide insight into how clients construct their reality while providing a method to operationalize clients' spiritual strengths. However, perhaps most importantly, spiritual lifemaps help practitioners provide more client-centered services.

References

Augustine. (354-430/1991). *Confessions* (H. Chadwick, Trans.). New York: Oxford University Press.

Azhar, M. Z., & Varma, S. L. (1995a). Religious psychotherapy as management of bereavement. *Acta Psychiatrica Scandinavica, 91,* 233-235.

Azhar, M. Z., & Varma, S. L. (1995b). Religious psychotherapy in depressive patients. *Psychotherapy and Psychosomatics, 63,* 165-168.

Azhar, M. Z., Varma, S. L., & Dharap, A. S. (1994). Religious psychotherapy in anxiety disorder patients. *Acta Psychiatrica Scandinavica, 90,* 1-2.

Bart, M. (1998). Spirituality in counseling finding believers. *Counseling Today, 41(6),* 1, 6.

Bullis, R. K. (1996). *Spirituality in social work practice.* Washington, DC: Taylor & Francis.

Burke, K. (1985). When words aren't enough [diss]. Union

for experimenting colleges and Universities.

Canda, E. R. (1997). Spirituality. In *1997 Supplement.* In R. L. Edwards (Ed.), *Encyclopedia of social work* (19, pp. 299-309). Washington, DC: NASW Press.

Canda, E. R., & Furman, L. D. (1999). *Spiritual diversity in social work practice.* New York: The Free Press.

Carroll, M. M. (1997). Spirituality and clinical social work: Implications of past and current perspectives. *Arete, 62(1),* 25-34.

Clark, G. (1993). *Augustine, the confessions.* New York: Cambridge University Press.

Cornett, C. (1992). Toward a more comprehensive personology: Integrating a spiritual perspective into social work practice. *Social Work, 37(2),* 101-102.

Derezotes, D. S. (1995). Spirituality and religiosity: Neglected factors in social work practice. *Arete, 20(1),* 1-15.

Doherty, W. J. (1999). Morality and spirituality in therapy. In F. Walsh (Ed.), *Spiritual resources in family therapy* (pp. 179-192). New York: Gilford Press.

Dor-Shav, N. K., Friedman, B., & Tcherbonogura, R. (1978). Identification, prejudice and aggression. *The Journal of Social Psychology, 104*, 217-222.

Ellerman, C. P. (1999). Pragmatic existential therapy. *Journal of Contemporary Psychotherapy, 29*(1), 49-64.

Ellison, C. G. (1993). Religious involvement and self-perception among Black Americans. *Social Forces, 71*(4), 1027-1055.

Ellison, C. G., & George, L., K. (1994). Religious involvement, social ties, and social support in a Southeastern community. *Journal for the Scientific Study of Religion, 33*(1), 46-61.

Ellison, C. G., & Levin, J. S. (1998). The religion-health connection: Evidence, theory, and future directions. *Health Education and Behavior, 25*(6), 700-720.

Elson, M. (1986). *Self psychology in clinical social work*. New York: W. W. Norton & Company.

Furman, L. D., & Chandy, J. M. (1994). Religion and spirituality: A long-neglected cultural component of rural social work practice. *Human Services in the Rural Environment, 17*(3/4), 21-26.

Furman, L. D., Perry, D., & Goldale, T. (1996). Interaction of Evangelical Christians and social workers in the rural environment. *Human Services in the Rural Environment, 19*(3), 5-8.

Gallup, G. J., & Castelli, J. (1989). *The people's religion: American faith in the 90's.* New York: Macmillan Publishing.

Ganje-Fling, M. A., & McCarthy, P. R. (1991). A comparative analysis of spiritual direction and psychotherapy. *Journal of Psychology and Theology, 19*(1), 103-117.

Gartner, J. (1996). Religious commitment, mental health, and prosocial behavior: A review of the empirical literature. In E. P. Shafranske (Ed.), *Religion and the clinical practice of psychology* (pp. 187-214). Washington, DC: American Psychological Association.

Haight, W. L. (1998). "Gathering the spirit" at first Baptist church: Spirituality as a protective factor in the lives of African American children. *Social Work, 43*(3), 213-221.

Hawkins, R. S., Tan, S.-Y., & Turk, A. A. (1999). Secular versus Christian inpatient cognitive-behavioral therapy programs: Impact on depression and spiritual well-being. *Journal of Psychology and 2Theology, 274*(4), 309-318.

Hepworth, D. H., & Larsen, J. A. (1993). *Direct Social Work Practice* (4). Pacific Grove, CA: Brooks/Cole Publishing.

Hodge, D. R. (2000a). Spiritual ecomaps: A new diagrammatic tool for assessing marital and family spirituality. *Journal of Marital and Family Therapy, 26*(1), 229-240.

Hodge, D. R. (2000b). Spirituality: Toward a theoretical framework. *Social Thought, 19*(4), 1-20.

Horovitz-Darby, E. G. (1994). *Spiritual art therapy.* Springfield, IL: Charles C Thomas.

Hoyt, M. F. (1998). Introduction. In M. F. Hoyt (Ed.), *The handbook of constructive therapies* (pp. 1-27). San Francisco: Jossey-Bass.

Jacobs, J. L. (1992). Religious ritual and mental health. In J. Schumaker (Ed.), *Religion and mental health* (pp. 291-

299). New York: Oxford University Press.

Joseph, M. (1998). The effects of strong religious beliefs on coping with stress. *Stress Medicine, 14*(4), 219-224.

Kahn, B. B. (1999). Art therapy with adolescents: Making it work for school counselors. *Professional School Counseling, 2*(4), 291-298.

Kennedy, J. E., Davis, R. C., & Talyor, B. G. (1998). Changes in spirituality and well-being among victims of sexual assault. *Journal for the Scientific Study of Religion, 37*(2), 322-328.

Kok, C. J., & Leskela, J. (1996). Solution-focused therapy in a psychiatric hospital. *Journal of Marital and Family Therapy, 22*(3), 397-406.

Lantz, J. (1998). Recollection in existential psychotherapy with older adults. *Journal of Clinical Geropsychology, 4*(1), 45-53.

McCullough, M. E., & Larson, D. B. (1999). Prayer. In W. R. Miller (Ed.), *Integrating spirituality into treatment* (pp. 85-110). Washington: American Psychological Association.

McNiff, S. (1992). *Art as medicine.* Boston: Shambhala.

Montgomery, C. (1994). Swimming upstream: The

strengths of women who survive homelessness. *Advanced Nursing Science*, *16*(3), 34-45.

Moon, B. L. (1994). *Introduction to art therapy*. Springfield, IL: Charles C Thomas.

Nason-Clark, N. (1998). Canadian Evangelical church women and responses to family violence. In M. Cousineau (Ed.), *Religion in a changing world* (pp. 57-65). Westport, CT: Praeger.

Nathanson, I., G. (1995). Divorce and women's spirituality. *Journal of Divorce and Remarriage*, *22*(3/4), 179-188.

Pargament, K. I. (1997). *The psychology of religion and coping*. New York: Guilford Press.

Perry, B. G. F. (1998). The relationship between faith and well-being. *Journal of Religion and Health*, *37*(2), 125-136.

Propst, L. R. (1996). Cognitive-behavioral therapy and the religious person. In E. P. Shafranske (Ed.), *Religion and the clinical practice of psychology* (pp. 391-407). Washington, DC: American Psychological Association.

Richards, P. S., & Bergin, A. E. (1997). *A spiritual strategy*. Washington, DC: American Psychological Association.

Richards, P. S., Owen, L., & Stein, S. (1993). A religiously oriented group counseling intervention for self-defeating perfectionism: A pilot study. *Counseling and Values*, *37*, 96-104.

Richert, A. J. (1999). Some thoughts on the integration of narrative and humanistic/existential approaches to psychotherapy. *Journal of Psychotherapy Integration*, *9*(2), 161-184.

Ronnau, J., & Poertner, J. (1993). Identification and use of strengths: A family system approach. *Children Today*, *22*(2), 20-23.

Saleebey, D. (Editor). (1997). *The strengths perspective* (2). New York: Longman.

Sheridan, M. J., & Amato-von Hemert, K. (1999). The role of religion and spirituality in social work education and practice: A survey of student views and experiences. *Journal of Social Work Education*, *35*(1), 125-141.

Sheridan, M. J., Bullis, R. K., Adcock, C. R., Berlin, S. D., & Miller, P. C. (1992). Practitioners' personal and professional attitudes and behaviors toward religion and spirituality: Issues for education and practice. *Journal of Social Work Education*, *28*(2), 190-203.

Strickland, L. (1994). Autobiographical interviewing and narrative analysis: An approach to psychosocial assessment. *Clinical Social Work Journal, 22*(1), 27-41.

Thayne, T. R. (1998). Opening space for clients' religious and spiritual values in therapy: A social constructionist perspective. In D. S. Becvar (Ed.), *The family, spirituality, and social work* (pp. 13-23). New York: Haworth Press.

Tracz, S. M., & Gehart-Brooks, D. R. (1999). The lifeline: Using art to illustrate history. *Journal of Family Psychotherapy, 10*(3), 61-63.

Ventis, W. L. (1995). The relationship between religion and mental health. *Journal of Social Issues, 51*(2), 33-48.

Weishaar, K. (1999). The visual life review as a therapeutic art framework with the terminally ill. *The Arts in Psychotherapy, 26*(3), 173-184.

Worthington, E. J., Kurusu, T., McCullough, M., & Sandage, S. (1996). Empirical research on religion and psychotherapeutic processes and outcomes: A 10-year review and research prospectus. *Psychological Bulletin, 119*(3), 448-487.

Zinnbauer, B. J., Pargament, K. I., Cole, B., Rye, M. S., Butter, E. M., Belavich, T. G., Hipp, K. M., Scott, A. B., & Kadar, J. L. (1997). Religion and spirituality: Unfuzzying the fuzzy. *Journal for the Scientific Study of Religion, 36*(4), 549-564.

CHAPTER FOUR

Spiritual Ecomaps: A Diagrammatic Tool for Assessing Marital and Family Spirituality in Space[4]

In the not too distant past, Prest and Keller suggested that the exploration of spirituality in marital and family therapy may be "more taboo than sex and death" (1993, p. 138). While there is still considerable work to be accomplished, growing interest exists among practitioners regarding tapping families' spiritual strengths (Anderson & Worthen, 1997). From a theoretical perspective, a number of authors have wrestled with the integration of spirituality into the therapeutic dialogue (Anderson & Worthen, 1997; Haug, 1998; Prest & Keller, 1993; Rey, 1997; Walsh, 1998; Weaver, Koenig, & Larson, 1997).

Bullis (1996) and Rey (1997) have suggested using diagrammatic instruments to explore clients' spirituality, such as genograms. Current approaches, however, generally conceptualize spirituality as a single factor among many that influence family functioning. While there is little doubt that this accurately reflects family dynamics in many cases, there may be instances when work with the client system requires a more conceptually focused spiritual instrument.

The Need

For many clients, religious beliefs and practices are particularly salient. For example, Bergin and Jensen (1990, p. 5) cite research indicating that 72% of the public agrees with the statement "my religious faith is the most important influence in my life. Further, among married couples and those with children, religious beliefs and practices hold increased levels of significance (Gallup & Castelli, 1989). Rural families can exhibit even higher degrees of

---

[4] Much of the material in this chapter appeared previously in an article written by D. R. Hodge entitled, "Spiritual ecomaps: A new diagrammatic tool for assessing marital and family spirituality" (2000) *Journal of Marital and Family Therapy, 26*(1), 229-240. This material is used in this book with the permission of the *Journal of Marital and Family Therapy.*

religiosity, to the point where God is understood to play a role equally significant to any family member (Furman & Chandy, 1994).

The growing accumulation of studies documenting the positive relationship between spirituality and family system functioning suggests the importance of a conceptually focused instrument. Various measures of spirituality and religion have been associated with marital adjustment (Hansen, 1992), stability (Call & Heaton, 1997), satisfaction (Gartner, 1996), sexual gratification (Payne, Bergin, Bielema, & Jenkins, 1991), and perception that one is better off as a result of being married (Wilson & Musick, 1996). Spirituality has been reported as an "essential ingredient" in long-term satisfying marriages (Kaslow & Robison, 1996). Conversely, regular church attendance is associated with lower incidence of marital problems that precipitate divorce (Amato & Rogers, 1997).

Spirituality has been associated with creating resilient families (Walsh, 1998), and enabling families to cope with being challenged by risk factors and to recover from crisis (McCubbin, McCubbin, Thompson, Han, & Allen, 1997). Religiosity, for example, is associated with positive adjustment outcomes in families who have a mentally challenged child (Rogers-Dulan, 1998) and with less anxiety and depression in families that encounter infant death, neonatal death, or stillbirth (Thearle, Vance, Najman, Embelton, & Foster, 1995).

The positive effects of spirituality extend throughout the family system, fostering lower instances of adolescent deviant behavior (Litchfield, Thomas, & Li, 1997) and alcohol use (Foshee & Hollinger, 1996). Among adolescents, religiosity is positively associated with prosocial values and behavior and negatively related to delinquency, substance abuse, premature sexual involvement, and suicide ideation and attempts (Donahue & Benson, 1995). Family worship that involves youths is associated with positive youth outcomes, including lower levels of materialism (Lee, Rice, & Gillespie, 1997).

As noted in chapter 1, the growing interest in utilizing clients' strengths is another factor highlighting the necessity of developing an instrument for spiritual assessment (Cowger, 1994; Hwang, Cowger, & Saleebey, 1998). Both solution-focused therapy and the strengths perspective focus on utilizing families' strengths in the therapeutic dialogue (Saleebey, 1997). Both frameworks share many of the same philosophical underpinnings, positing that clients can become overwhelmed with problems and deficits and, consequently, can neglect resources or strengths. These frameworks understand social reality to be co-constructed, leading to a collaborative approach in therapy in which a blending of ideas and strategies between the client and therapist fosters client self-expertise (Kok & Leskela, 1996; Kuehl, 1995).

Therapists may encourage their clients to develop an awareness of resources that can be applied to presenting problems. Solutions drawn from clients' resources are held to be more empowering and more likely to be applied than strategies derived from traditional problem-centered frameworks. Specific to solution-focused brief therapy is the development of a number of interventions such as the miracle question, the scaling question, and identifying exceptions to the problem.[5] (Kok & Leskela, 1996; Kuehl, 1995).

As the above empirical findings documenting the beneficial nature of spirituality have gained wider audience, interest in accessing spirituality has increased. Solution-oriented therapists in particular may be interested in exploring a largely neglected family resource. Yet, as Ronnau and Poertner (1993) have noted, without a reliable tool for finding clients' strengths, practitioners tend to leave strengths untapped.

---

[5] "Miracle questions" enable clients to visualize how their lives would be different if suddenly they did not have to deal with their presenting problem any longer. An example would be, "Suppose you were sleeping tonight and a miracle happens. You wake up in the morning and your problem is gone. How would you know the miracle had happened? How would your life be different?

"Scaling questions" provide insight into clients' perceptions. An example of a scaling question would be, On a scale of 1 to 10, where 1 stands for "I have the worst possible marriage relationship in the history of humankind and 10 stands for I have the best possible marriage relationship in humankind," what number between 1 and 10 would you assign to your marriage relationship?

"Exception finding questions" are used to identify times when a problem would normally occur but for some reason does not. An example of an exception finding question would be, I would be interested in knowing about the times when the problem is just a little bit better, or the problem is gone, even for a short time.

The philosophies underlying the strengths perspective and solution-oriented brief therapy also imply that other therapeutic modalities can beneficially incorporate an exploration of strengths to counterbalance the examination of problems and deficits. Indeed, it is easy to envision a number of circumstances in which practitioners would desire richer information in the purview of spirituality than current methods yield. For example, in many families, especially those from rural areas, the spiritual belief system may be the most important aspect of family (Furman & Chandy, 1994). While other dynamics certainly exist and are important to explore, in numerous instances, spirituality is the most important dimension of family functioning. In such cases, an extensive data set detailing current functioning is crucial. Even in situations where spirituality plays a lesser role in a family's life, it may still be a vital strength that can be used to address problems through the use of spiritual interventions, a growing number of which have been empirically validated (Jacobs, 1992; Pargament, 1997; Propst, 1996; Worthington, Kurusu, McCullough, & Sandage, 1996).

Ecomaps and Genograms

Ecological maps, or ecomaps, were developed by Hartman in 1975 as a means of depicting the ecological system that encompasses a family or individual (Hartman, 1995). While genograms depict families over time, ecomaps portray them in space. In other words, maps delineate the major systems that are currently part of a family's life as well as a family's relationship to those systems.

By focusing on current functioning, maps provide an important supplement to genograms, which highlight past history. Ideally, the two instruments complement one another. Due to ecomaps' unique emphasis upon current functioning, however, they offer particular advantages. For example, clients who are skeptical of exploring past functioning usually understand the need to examine their current relationship to environment systems in the course of addressing their current presenting problems. Also, in today's outcome-based managed care climate, a present focus offering a timely transition to interventions can be an asset (Kok & Laskela, 1996).

Using ecomaps is highly congruent with a solution-oriented approach. Ecomaps, in contrast with the historical orientation of genograms, shift the emphasis away from the family system and related subsystems to environmental systems. By concentrating on the current systems that affect family functioning, the practitioner transmits the message that intergenerational deficits are not the primary area of concern. Although problems can be explored within the context of an ecomap, this approach alters the central ethos. In addition to shifting the focus to external systems, ecomaps lend themselves to a cooperative therapeutic alliance in much the same way that genograms do, as both the practitioner and the family members work together to fill out the diagrammatic instrument (Hartman, 1995).

According to Hartman (1995), extensive testing by the Michigan Department of Social Services with parents who experienced a mandated child placement outside their home has demonstrated the effectiveness of ecomaps. As one would expect, practitioners noted that parents were angry and self-protective following placements due to abuse or neglect. Yet, almost without exception, parents became engaged in the therapeutic process through the use of maps. Dramatic decreases in defensiveness were generally reported, along with enhanced therapeutic rapport (Hartman, 1995).

A modified version of the ecomap may be particularly helpful in operationalizing the significant aspects of family spirituality. Spirituality, especially within a number of theistic, and more specifically, numerous Christian traditions, is often understood in relational terms, a key dimension highlighted by maps. Furthermore, ecomaps' ability to explore environmental systems dovetails nicely with the social support resources in most religious traditions.

Constructing an Ecomap

As Hartman (1995) has illustrated, the ecomap is a pen and paper depiction of the family in existential relationship to environmental systems. The ecomap uses standard genogram format to sketch family relationships and key events (McGoldrick, Gerson, & Shellenberger, 1999). A large circle encompasses the current members of the family household.

Figure 1 (pg. 61) depicts how a helping professional might draw a family comprised of a father and mother with a 9-year-old son. The mother was divorced three years prior to her current marriage. The union produced one daughter, who lived with the

Figure 1

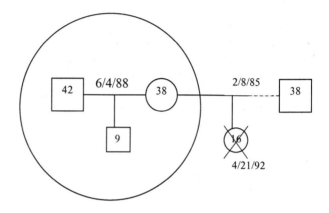

father after the dissolution of the marriage. The solid line between the mother and daughter indicates a continuous relationship until the daughter's death in 1992.

The heart of the traditional ecomap is the connection between the nuclear family system and various environmental systems or domains (e.g., extended family, health care, recreation, school, work, etc.). Like the family system, the practitioner draws these as circles, with the names of the respective systems placed inside. A line connects the family system with the environmental systems. The thickness of the line represents the strength of the relational connection, with a dashed line depicting the most tenuous connection. A jagged line describes a conflicted relationship. Arrows superimposed on the lines indicate the flow of resources, energy, or interest. The practitioner can write descriptions along the connecting lines or beside the environmental system depicted by the circle. Descriptions can also serve as alternatives to arrows or in addition to them. The practitioner can draw connections to the family as a whole, to individual members, or both, depending upon the relationship.

As is readily apparent, the central problem in transforming traditional ecomaps into their spiritual counterparts lies in the environmental systems. While diagramming the family system remains unchanged, new, specifically spiritual domains must be developed for the environmental section of the spiritual ecomap. A related problem is fostering a dialogue of sufficient depth to reveal the salient aspects of spiritual life. Because practitioners tend to have minimal training in spiritual issues, an anthropological framework designed to facilitate understanding of spiritual issues may be especially useful (Weaver et al., 1997). Accordingly, the next section develops a multidimensional spiritual anthropology, based on Nee's (1968) conceptualization of spirit. As Bullis (1996) noted, a spiritual anthropology provides the foundation for understanding the spiritual element of personal ontology. More specifically, it provides the theoretical rationale for making particular inquiries, understanding the resulting data, and incorporating specific domains in a spiritual ecomap.

A Multidimensional Spiritual Anthropology

African, Eastern, and Western spiritual formation traditions hold the view that humans are comprised of more than the personality functions of affect, cognition, and volition, in conjunction with soma. In addition to these functions, there is a transpersonal element that is fundamental to human ontology. This element is referred to as *pneuma*, or spirit.

As discussed in chapter 2, spirituality writer Watchman Nee (1968) conceptualizes spirit as an integrative unity comprised of communion, conscience, and intuition. These three dimensions interact with and influence one another and are integrally interwoven with affect, cognition, and volition. Yet, while integrated, they are discrete enough to be distinguished. Just as cognition can be distinguished from affect, for example, so the three dimensions of the spirit can be distinguished from one another.

Communion refers to the capacity to bond and relate with both spiritual beings and humans. Mystics from myriad religious traditions testify to a rich, deep sense of communion with God, for example. Religious conversions, spiritual awakenings, and ecstatic prayer also express this dimension of the spirit. Similarly, many individuals report contact with various transpersonal beings such as angels, demons, evil spirits, lower-order gods, saints, and recently deceased relatives (Morse & Perry, 1994).

Cross-sectional research indicates that more than 40% of the general public admits to a mystical experience or contact with transpersonal beings (Gallup & Castelli, 1989; Levin, 1994). Further, approximately 50% of bereaved individuals experience the presence of the recently departed family member (Lindstrom, 1995). Evidence suggests these experiences are often life changing in nature and continue to inform one's actions indefinitely (Fitchett, 1993; Morse & Perry, 1994).

As stated above, communion also includes the ability to connect deeply with people. It is especially prominent among family members and members of one's religious community. It is also marked by a sense of being kindred spirits in certain friendships (Nee, 1968). This sense of connectedness, it has been suggested, is transmuted beyond the individualistic to the universal in spiritual individuals, manifested in a compassionate concern for humankind (Elkins, et al., 1988; Genia, 1990).

Conscience is associated with morality (Nee, 1968) It can be conceptualized as humankind's ethical guidance system. At an intuitive level, beyond the scope of cognition, it informs one as to what is just and fair and what is immoral and nefarious. The spiritual formation tradition also holds that a close relationship with the Transcendent is predicated upon following the promptings of the conscience. Accordingly, while external factors shape conscience and consequently change it over time, spiritual individuals live in a manner consistent with their interior value framework (Genia, 1990). When this internal standard is transgressed, metaphysical and psychological consequences generally result. For example, guilt and shame are byproducts of diverging, even involuntarily, from this guidance system. While each person's conscience is unique, tailored by individual, social, and cultural factors, there are also universal, transcultural norms (Nee, 1968).

Intuition is the ability to sense or to have insights that do not come through normal cognitive channels and is a form of knowledge. Hunches concerning the advisability of a certain course of action, sudden impressions to pray for someone, creative flashes of insight, and déjà vu are examples of intuition. Clients often understand intuition to be a spiritual strength (Krill, 1990; Nee, 1968). The key factor is that impressions arrive at the conscious level directly, bypassing normal information-processing channels.

Premonitions involving impending disaster or death are another manifestation of intuition and occur more frequently than many practitioners are aware. For example, one study found that approximately 20% of parents who lost a child due to sudden infant death syndrome had a premonition of the child's coming death (Morse & Perry, 1994). In the control group that lost no children, only 3% of parents experienced premonitions. Further, there was a sharp difference in the nature of premonitions reported. For parents who lost a child, the premonition tended to be characterized by a hyperreality that made them unforgettable. For some individuals, the premonitions had a positive effect upon their emotional well-being while for others the effect was negative. However, regardless of whether the premonitions were salutary or deleterious, they engendered a high degree of emotional impact (Morse & Perry, 1994).

A Spiritual Ecomap

In addition to providing an overview of spiritual functioning, the spiritual anthropology, in association with collateral material from the spiritual formation tradition, provides the necessary environmental systems to complete a spiritual ecomap. The three dimensions of the spirit—communion, conscience, and intuition—are manifested most clearly in one's relationship with God and in significant human relationships. In regard to the latter, the most important relationships are as follows: family of origin, particularly parents; individuals within the religious community; and spiritual leaders. While patterns are often evident in the various metaphysical and human relationships, there are frequently marked differences as well, warranting the exploration of all areas in families where spirituality plays an important role.

Figure 2 (see pg. 66)demonstrates what an empty map might look like. In addition to the above constructs, two additional domains are included, "Transpersonal Beings" and "Rituals." The former is included due the prevalence of contact with these entities (Gallup & Castelli, 1989; Levin, 1994) and the enduring significance individuals attach to such encounters (Fitchett, 1993; Morse & Perry, 1994). In fact, due to the possibility of numerous encounters with discrete transpersonal beings (e.g., angels, demons, evil spirits, lower-order Hindu gods, saints, relatives that have recently died and the different relational characteristics of each type of encounter, it may be appropriate to add other domains to the map that represent the various relational dynamics, in accordance with the experiences relayed in the clinical setting. It should be mentioned that many transpersonal encounters are mutually exclusive in various traditions (e.g., Catholics are unlikely to discuss encounters with lower-order gods), limiting the number of required domains.

Rituals refer to codified spiritual practices. One of the stronger empirical findings in the purview of religion is the effectiveness of spiritually based rituals as coping strategies for handling stressful life events (Pargament, 1997; Worthington, et al., 1996). Rituals serve to reinforce the sense of attachment to others as well as to the Transcendent. The sense of bonding facilitates a cathartic response through which painful emotions engendered by stressful events can be brought to consciousness and relived or expressed, which in turn fosters well-being (Jacobs, 1992).

The domains listed in the spiritual ecomap can be introduced in any number of fashions. Some practitioners may wish to follow a developmental framework by starting with the family of origin. Others may feel that the client's relationship with God is the natural starting point. Introducing the instrument as a tool to identify spiritual strengths or resources and beginning with the Rituals domain allows clients to operationalize the strengths based phi

<u>Figure 2</u>

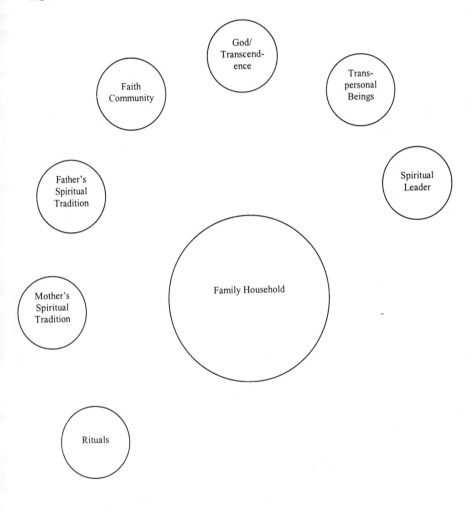

losophical principles underlying the instrument from its initial use, however. Further, it allows time for the therapist to build rapport before broaching more sensitive areas such as the Transpersonal beings domain.

In practice, the God/Transcendence domain can be tightly woven into the discussion of discrete rituals, and the domains may be filled out consecutively or even concurrently. It is suggested that the former be placed at the top of the map in order to signify the preeminence of this relationship for most clients, while rituals are placed at the bottom, signifying their foundational role. One may wish to change the placement of the various domains in keeping with the perceptions of clients, however, so that the resulting map reflects clients' spiritual perceptions. A format is offered directly below for discussing the various systems with families. It moves from the exploration of the relatively informal domain, rituals, to progressively more personal domains of family members' spiritual universe.

A series of questions can assist in accessing the following systems. Three points should be kept in mind regarding these questions. First, the practitioner's empathic responses are often critical in fostering an open exploration of what can be a very personal area. Second, tentative, open-ended phrasings (e.g., "I wonder if you could explain . . ." , "I am curious about . . .") frequently yield richer information and foster an enhanced therapeutic atmosphere. Practitioners should constantly monitor the clinical relationship in light of the question being asked and incorporate appropriate nonjudgmental phrasing.

Finally, the question set below is based upon my experience, informed by the material presented in the previous section and supplemented by material drawn from an eclectic mix of sources. Accordingly, practitioners will want to tailor the material in keeping with their own knowledge base while adapting the questions to be as culturally sensitive as possible. For example, in place of God or Transcendence, one might substitute Allah when working with Muslims, Almighty with Hindus, God the Father with Christians, a system of spiritually oriented teachings with Buddhists, and so on. Similarly, one would avoid asking Muslims, with their strong belief in one God, whether they have had encounters with lower gods, a question appropriate for a Hindu family.

Spiritual Domains

Rituals. "What particular rituals or practices nurture your spirituality/family life? Are there specific symbols that are spiritually significant to you? What rituals/practices facilitate coping with hardship, illness, trials?"

God/Transcendent. "Describe your relationship to God. Have there been times when you have felt deep intimacy (distance) with the divine? What facilitates this sense of closeness (distance)? How does the state of your conscience affect your relationship with God? How does your spirituality relate to life's difficulties (joys)? How do you deal with transgressions/misdeeds that violate your conscience? How does your relationship with the Transcendent affect your relationship with others? What sort of fruit does it produce? Have you received premonitions or intuitive insights from God concerning life events?"

Religious community. "What is your level of involvement in religious communities (churches, Mosques, small groups, synagogues, temples, etc.)? What are their primary religious/spiritual beliefs, and how reflective are they of your own beliefs? What sort of atmosphere (i.e., cold, warm, conflicted, open, etc.) does your faith community transmit?"

Spiritual leader. "Describe your relationship with those you consider to hold a position of spiritual leadership with your family (i.e., pastor, priest, rabbi, spiritual elder, guide, director, etc.). What sort of emotional word picture would encapsulate the relationship? Is there a link between this relationship and the relationship to your parents' spiritual tradition?"

Parents' spiritual tradition. "What was the religious tradition you grew up in, and how did your family express its spiritual beliefs? What sort of personal spiritual experiences stand out to you during your years at home? How much autonomy did you experience within the family's spiritual tradition? What were the differences and similarities between your parents' expression of faith? How did those differences in beliefs/practices affect you and your relationship with either parent? How have you transitioned or matured from the spirituality of your youth, and how would you describe your current relationship to your family's (father's/mother's) traditions?"

Transpersonal beings. "Have you had encounters with transpersonal beings such as angels, demons, evil spirits? Did you ever feel the intervention of a saint (angel/lower-order god) on your behalf? Have you had experiences with relatives who have died? How would you describe these encounters?"

Additional areas to explore include creative insights, mystical experiences, and depth of intimacy and degree of involvement with other individuals. The ultimate goal is to delineate any relationship that affects the family's spirituality. As is the case with marriages and divorces, specific, formative spiritual experiences can be briefly sketched or illustrated. Dates, along with a brief description if necessary, can be written either next to the appropriate environmental system or on the line representing the nature of the relationship.

A final point warrants emphasizing. The heart of the exploration should be the meaning families attach to the various systems in their spiritual universe. Diagrammatic instruments tend to concretize. Accordingly, there is a danger the tool may drive the dialogue by leading the practitioner to focus on recording specific, concrete events, such as spiritual awakenings, that are easily depicted. The intent, however, is to use the instrument's strength to specify the meanings families associate with the events. In other words, the content of the relational aspect between the various domains and family members should be the crux of the clinical dialogue.

A Case Study

Figure 3 (see pg. 70) depicts the use of a spiritual ecomap with a relatively complex, although not uncommon, family. It features the family discussed in Figure 1 animated by evangelical Christianity and common relational associations. The evangelical tradition was chosen for the following reasons: practitioners are unlikely to be personal adherents of this tradition (Weaver, et al., 1997); the tradition has been under-researched, accentuating most therapists' unfamiliarity with evangelicalism (Larson, Sherrill, & Lyons, 1994); and it is the largest discrete faith tradition in the United States, comprising approximately 25% of the population (Gallup & Castelli, 1989; Richards & Bergin, 1997).

As the heavy connecting line and arrow denote, the family is involved in a local evangelical Christian church, which everyone strongly perceives to be a source of strength for the entire family. The family also participates in regular rituals derived from their religious belief system, such as family nights, prayer times, scripture storytelling, and so on, which all members enjoy.

Figure 3

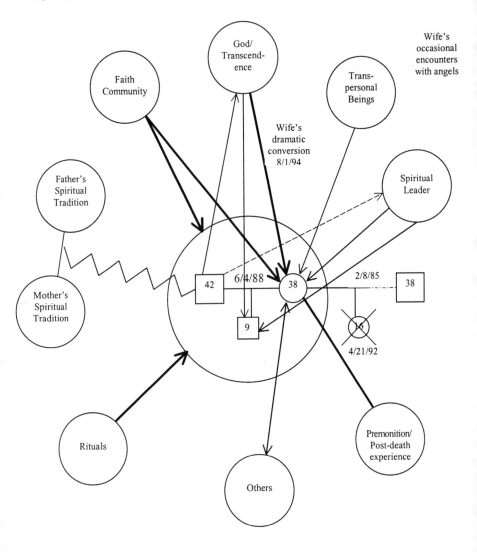

The husband professes a dislike for the conservative Protestant tradition of his parents, which he experienced as overly rigid, and contrasts it sharply with the informality of the evangelical Christian fellowship the family currently attends. He has connected with other men in the fellowship through participation in events such as Promise Keepers, which he feels have made him a better husband and father. His relationship with God is somewhat strained, however. God is viewed as placing too many rules and regulations on him. He does not hold the pastor in high regard and often considers his sermons boring.

The wife grew up in a relatively secular family and had little interest in metaphysical issues until she received a strong premonition of her daughter's impending death. This event, along with a post-death visionary encounter, led her on a spiritual search that culminated in a dramatic spiritual conversion approximately two years after her daughter's death. Subsequently, she has never questioned the existence of God. It was these spiritual experiences that sparked the family's involvement in a religious community.

The subsequent relationship with God is a major strength in the wife's life, fostering personal forgiveness and healing concerning her previous divorce and increased coping resources in general. While the whole family enjoys their church, she finds it an especially nourishing environment. She frequently senses the presence of God in daily affairs and has experienced events in which she believes angels have intervened to thwart impending disasters. She is extensively involved in the lives of others in the broader community, participating in a number of social action groups. While such engagement is often draining, it also provides many rewarding experiences. Like her son, she has a positive relationship with the pastor.

The son enjoys the atmosphere in church and has developed a number of close friends from within the fellowship. He admires the pastor as an adult who regularly takes the time to inquire what transpired during his week. The family rituals are especially enjoyable for him, and he views God as a benevolent protector who cares for him.

Uses Of A Spiritual Ecomap

As is the case with a traditional ecomap, spiritual maps can be used for assessment, planning, and intervention. The most widely used approach to spiritual assessment is the process of taking of a spiritual history (see chapter 2), a method analogous to taking a family history. While this approach can yield rich amounts of data, it lacks a framework for organizing the resulting data in a useful format. A spiritual ecomap can be employed to organize the information visually, or it can stand alone as an assessment instrument.

The latter approach is particularly important in cases where practitioners are uncomfortable addressing spiritual areas or encounter a spiritual tradition that is outside their experience. By its very nature as a collective instrument focusing on environmental resources instead of inner deficits, the ecomap fosters a partnership between the two parties, mitigating the unease of both participants. The family provides the information, often in a collateral seating arrangement in which the family and the practitioner are seated beside one another with the map as the focal point, and the practitioner fills in the responses. Maps, in conjunction with empathy and genuine curiosity, provide a means of probing a family's existential reality even if the practitioner has little previous experience in the area. Further, the process of completing the map allows time for the practitioner to gain a degree of familiarity and ease with the family's spiritual tradition before considering interventions.

The pictorial representation of the family's current spiritual relationships fosters an easy transition from assessment to planning. Spiritual strengths can be clearly identified and harnessed to tackle problems in other areas. Similarly, because spirituality expresses itself in relationship to other individuals, tenuous relationships are also delineated, and their physical depiction suggests interventions planned to alleviate the difficulties.

For example, in a manner consistent with solution-oriented perspectives, the practitioner can ask clients how their spiritual strengths can be used to address their difficulties. Similarly, the practitioner can suggest new behaviors that divert attention away from problems and establish productive new patterns. If attendance at a Promise Keepers small group ameliorates marital tensions in the days following participation, for instance, can he go twice a week? The practitioner might also investigate the dynamics that foster exceptions to the problem after attendance at a Promise Keepers meeting. Once the beneficial dynamics have been identified, exploration could occur regarding how they might be imported into the marriage in other ways. practitioner can explore with clients empirically-validated spiritual interventions such as prayer, meditation, forgiveness, and cognitive restructuring using spiritual content revealed in the ecomap (Jacobs, 1992; Propst, 1996; Worthington, et al., 1996). Homework assignments can strengthen these interventions. For example, a family member wrestling with depression could meditate on a particular therapeutically oriented set of scriptures on noticing the onset of symptoms and could then record the results.

Spiritual ecomaps can also demonstrate to the family how their situation has changed since the start of therapy. A key tenet of solution-focused perspectives is the necessity of reinforcing the perception that change is occurring (Kok & Leskela, 1996). Since change is often difficult to quantify, the visible depiction of altered relationships on a newly constructed map can be compared to the original as a means of clearly demonstrating the changes that have occurred. Such interventions can encourage families at critical junctions or can be used as a positive way of concluding the therapeutic relationship.

Regardless of its point of use in the therapeutic continuum, the map's primary value lies in its ability to visually organize and present concurrently not only a great amount of factual information but the relationships between the various systems (Hartman, 1995). The resulting visual depiction can have a profound impact upon family members, fostering deeper understanding and motivation to address difficulties. For example, in the family profiled above, the differences between the husband's and the wife's spiritual experiences are clearly evident. Further, the nature of the differences may not be apparent to others or even the couple themselves since both are involved in church activities and family based rituals and have relationships with God.

Spiritual ecomaps can be particularly efficacious in families where spirituality is a salient factor. However, in families where it plays a lesser role, traditional ecomaps, or perhaps other diagrammatic instruments such as genograms, may be more appropriate. In some cases, a traditional ecomap incorporating a domain titled "spiritual resources" may represent the most appropriate approach.

Conclusion

Developing a clear and concise understanding of a family's relationship to spiritual systems is an area of growing interest among helping professionals. Not only does the empirical evidence suggest this is a positive advance, but by addressing what numerous clients hold as a central constituent of their lives, practitioners send the message that they value and respect this component. Indeed, what sort of message had been sent by helping professionals' long neglect of spirituality?

Thus, in addition to exploring what may be a family's primary strength, assessing spirituality embodies the strengths and solution-oriented perspectives by tapping into potential resources in an area that often informs every facet of existence. To ignore this area is to engage clients in the therapeutic milieu with a distorted understanding of the dynamics that inform their functioning. Spiritual ecomaps offer practitioners an instrument that effectively operationalizes this vital subjective area in a clinically useful manner.

References

Amato, P. R., & Rogers, S. J. (1997). A longitudinal study of marital problems and subsequent divorce. *Journal of Marriage and the Family, 59,* 612–624.

Anderson, D., & Worthen, D. (1997). Exploring a fourth dimension: Spirituality as a resource for the couple therapist. *Journal of Marital and Family Therapy, 23*(1), 3–12.

Bergin, A. E., & Jensen, J. P. (1990). Religiosity of psychotherapists: A national survey. *Psychotherapy, 27*(1), 3–7.

Bullis, R. K. (1996). *Spirituality in social work practice.* Washington, DC: Taylor & Francis.

Call, V. R., & Heaton, T. B. (1997). Religious influences on marital stability. *Journal for the Scientific Study of Religion, 36*(3), 382–392.

Cowger, C. D. (1994). Assessing client strengths: Clinical assessments for client empowerment. *Social Work, 39*(3), 262–268.

Donahue, M., & Benson, P. L. (1995). Religion and the well-being of adolescents. *Journal of Social Issues, 51*(2), 145–160.

Elkins, D. N., Hedstrom, L. J., Hughes, L. L., Leaf, J. A., & Saunders, C. (1988). Toward a humanistic-phenomenological spirituality: Definition, description and measurement.

Journal of Humanistic Psychology, 28(4), 5-18.

Fitchett, G. (1993). *Assessing spiritual needs*. Minneapolis: Augsburg.

Foshee, V. A., & Hollinger, B. R. (1996). Maternal religiosity, adolescent social bonding, and adolescent alcohol use. *Journal of Early Adolescence, 16*(4), 451-468.

Furman, L. D., & Chandy, J. M. (1994). Religion and spirituality: A long-neglected cultural component of rural social work practice. *Human Services in the Rural Environment, 17*(3/4), 21-26.

Gallup, G. J., & Castelli, J. (1989). *The people's religion: American faith in the 90's*. New York: Macmillan.

Gartner, J. (1996). Religious commitment, mental health, and prosocial behavior: A review of the empirical literature. In E. P. Shafranske (Ed.), *Religion and the clinical practice of psychology* (pp. 187-214). Washington, DC: American Psychological Association.

Genia, V. (1990). Religious development: A synthesis and reformulation. *Journal of Religion and Health, 29*(2), 85-99.

Hansen, G. L. (1992). Religion and marital adjustment. In J. F. Schumaker (Ed.), *Relig-*

ion and mental health (pp. 189-199). New York: Oxford University Press.

Hartman, A. (1995). Diagrammatic assessment of family relationships. *Families in Society: The Journal of Contemporary Human Services, 76*(2), 111-122.

Haug, I. (1998). Including a spiritual dimension in family therapy: Ethical considerations. *Contemporary Family Therapy: An International Journal, 20*(2), 181-194.

Hwang, S. C., Cowger, C., D., & Saleebey, D. (1998). Utilizing strengths in assessment/another view: Is strengths-based practice becoming more common? *Families in Society: The Journal of Contemporary Human Services, 97*(1), 25-31.

Jacobs, J. L. (1992). Religious ritual and mental health. In J. Schumaker (Ed.), *Religion and mental health* (pp. 291-299). New York: Oxford University Press.

Kaslow, F., & Robison, J. A. (1996). Long-term satisfying marriages: Perceptions contributing factors. *The American Journal of Family Therapy, 24*(2), 153-170.

Kok, C. J., & Leskela, J. (1996). Solution-focused therapy in a psychiatric hospital. *Journal of Marital and Family Therapy, 22*, 397-406.

Krill, D. F. (1990). *Practice wisdom. Sage human services guides* (Vol. 62). London: Sage.

Kuehl, B. (1995). The solution-oriented genogram: A collaborative approach. *Journal of Marital and Family Therapy, 21,* 239–250.

Larson, D. B., Sherrill, K. A., & Lyons, J. S. (1994). Neglect and misuse of the R word. In J. S. Levin (Ed.), *Religion in aging and health* (pp. 178–195). London: Sage.

Lee, J. W., Rice, G. T., & Gillespie, V. B. (1997). Family worship patterns and their correlation with adolescent behavior and beliefs. *Journal for the Scientific Study of Religion, 36*(3), 272–381.

Levin, J., S. (1994). Investigating the epidemiologic effects of religious experience. In J. S. Levin (Ed.), *Religion in aging and health: Theoretical foundations and methodological frontiers* (pp. 3–17). Thousand Oaks, CA: Sage.

Lindstrom, T. C. (1995). Experiencing the presence of the dead: Discrepancies in "the sensing experience" and their psychological concomitants. *Omega, 31*(1), 11–21.

Litchfield, A. W., Thomas, D. L., & Li, B. D. (1997). Dimensions of religiosity as mediators on the relations between parenting and adolescent deviant behavior. *Journal of Adolescent Research, 12*(2), 199–226.

McCubbin, H. I., McCubbin, M. A., Thompson, A. I., Han, S. Y., & Allen, C. T. (1997). Families under stress: What makes them resilient. *Journal of Family and Consumer Sciences, 89*(3), 2–12.

McGoldrick, M., Gerson, R., & Shellenberger, S. (1999). *Genograms: Assessment and Intervention* (2nd ed.). New York: Norton.

Morse, M., & Perry, P. (1994). *Parting visions.* New York: Villard.

Nee, W. (1968). *The spiritual man* (Vol. 1–3). New York: CFP.

Pargament, K. I. (1997). *The psychology of religion and coping.* New York: Guilford.

Payne, I. R., Bergin, A. E., Bielema, K. A., & Jenkins, P. H. (1991). Review of religion and mental health: Prevention and enhancement of psychosocial functioning. *Prevention in Human Services, 9*(2), 11–40.

Prest, L. A., & Keller, J. F. (1993). Spirituality and family therapy: Spiritual beliefs, myths and metaphors. *Journal of Marital and Family Therapy, 19,* 137–148.

Propst, L. R. (1996). Cognitive-behavioral therapy and the religious person. In E. P. Shafranske (Ed.), *Religion and the clinical practice of psychology* (pp. 391–407). Washington, DC: American Psychological Association.

Rey, L. D. (1997). Religion as invisible culture: Knowing about and knowing with. *Journal of Family Social Work, 2*(2), 159–177.

Richards, P. S., & Bergin, A. E. (1997). *A spiritual strategy.* Washington, DC: American Psychological Association.

Rogers-Dulan, J. (1998). Religious connectedness among urban African American families who have a child with disabilities. *Mental Retardation, 36*(2), 91–103.

Ronnau, J., & Poertner, J. (1993). Identification and use of strengths: A family system approach. *Children Today, 22*(2), 20–23.

Thearle, M. J., Vance, J. C., Najman, J. M., Embelton, G., & Foster, W. J. (1995). Church attendance, religious affiliation and parental responses to sudden infant death, neonatal death and stillbirth. *Omega, 31*(1), 51–58.

Walsh, F. (1998). Beliefs, spirituality, and transcendence. In M. McGoldrick (Ed.), *Revisioning family therapy: Race, culture, and transcendence in clinical practice* (pp. 62–77). New York: Guilford.

Weaver, A. J., Koenig, H. G., & Larson, D. B. (1997). Marriage and family therapists and the clergy: A need for clinical collaboration, training, and research. *Journal of Marital and Family Therapy, 23*, 13–25.

Wilson, J., & Musick, M. (1996). Religion and marital dependency. *Journal for the Scientific Study of Religion, 35*(1), 30–40.

Worthington, E. J., Kurusu, T., McCullough, M., & Sandage, S. (1996). Empirical research on religion and psychotherapeutic processes and outcomes: A 10-year review and research prospectus. *Psychological Bulletin, 119*(3), 448–487.

CHAPTER FIVE

Spiritual Genograms: A Generational Approach to Assessing Spirituality[6]

There are a number of reasons for adopting a generational approach for spiritual assessment. Wuthnow's (1999) ethnographic study (N = 200) on religious perceptions led him to conclude that there are at least three important generational aspects involved in the transmission of spiritual and religious values. First, there is the direct influence that grandparents have with their children and grandchildren in settings where several generations live together in the same household. Second, in situations in which grandparents do not live in the household, they indirectly shape perceptions through the memories they evoke, especially in cases where at least one of the grandparents was noted for piety. Finally, gender differences are also relevant, since mothers and grandmothers frequently play a decisive role in childhood religious experiences.

In most cases, families are successful in passing on their values and beliefs. Bengtson and Harootyan's (1994) nationally representative study (N = 1500) on intergenerational linkages found that most respondents felt their opinions were either "similar" or "very similar" to those of their parents. Likewise, O'Connor and associates' (1999) 24-year follow-up study (N = 206) of religious behaviors and attitudes found that 68% of respondents still self-identified as members of their original denomination.

Conversely, spiritually related issues can be a source of intergenerational conflict. Clarke and associates' (1999, p. 267) analysis of the Longitudinal Study of Generations data file (N = 1137) found that "religious beliefs were often mentioned as areas of con-

---

6 Much of the material in this chapter appeared previously in an article written by D. R. Hodge entitled, Spiritual genograms: A generational approach to assessing spirituality (2001). *Families in Society, 82*(1), 35-48.This material is used in this book with the permission of the *Families in Society.*

flict." An adult child may, for example, experience a spiritual awakening, leave her parents' denomination that was perceived to be spiritually lifeless, and join a new denomination that is perceived to be more spiritually alive. To summarize, while the individualistic perspective makes an important contribution, each person is imbedded in a particular family structure.

Family-of-origin continues to inform beliefs and experiences, regardless of whether individuals negotiate a place for themselves within their family's tradition or exercise their right to convert to another faith tradition. Thus, it is important to develop generationally-based assessment procedures that are more congruent with the person-in-environment approach that has traditionally informed helping professions such as social work. A modified version of the traditional genogram would seem to present an ideal vehicle for this task. Traditional genograms are widely used and have been adapted to serve a number of discrete uses (McGoldrick, Gerson & Shellenberger, 1999).

A spiritual genogram is an assessment instrument specifically designed to identify and operationalize the spiritual and religious strengths that exist in clients' family systems.

Charting the family

The first step in constructing a spiritual genogram is to delineate the basic family structure over three generations (Frame, 2000a). Grandparents, parents, aunts, uncles, cousins, siblings, nieces and nephews are depicted, along with significant dates, such as births, marriages, divorces, remarriages, and deaths, as in a typical genogram. Some practitioners may also find it helpful to symbolize the quality of the relationships, noting conflict, closeness, distance, etc. McGoldrick, Gerson and Shellenberger (1999) and Stanion, Papadopoulos and Bor (1997) provide, respectively, book and article length overviews of basic genogram construction.

Family members, however, are not the only actors in a client's spiritual history. Indeed, many religious traditions conceptualize themselves as a form of spiritual, as opposed to biological, family. Consequently, there may be distantly related or even unrelated individuals who played a role of spiritual import equal to any person in the client's immediate constellation of relatives over the course of time (Hardy & Laszloffy, 1995). These individuals can also be listed on the spiritual genogram (Bullis, 1990). Thus, to supplement the traditional squares representing males and circles denoting females, triangles can be used to designate individuals who have played major spiritual roles but are not members of the immediate biological family.

Color Coding Denominational Affiliation and Religious Preference

Drawing pencils of various hues can indicate clients' spiritual orientation, their spiritual and religious beliefs or spiritual cosmology, on the basic genogram (Lewis, 1989). Color coding provides a graphic "color snapshot" of the overall spiritual composition of clients' families, which in turn suggests a variety of initial hypotheses about clients' present spiritual reality (Hardy & Laszloffy, 1995). For example, a couple's spiritual genogram that consists of a single color on one side and is multicolored on the other can highlight contrasting spiritual orientations.

More specifically, the square representing a grandfather who was a devout Southern Baptist could be colored red while the circle depicting his wife, a member of the Assemblies of God, might be colored orange. Similarly, a son who is a Muslim might be colored brown and his Roman Catholic wife green. Other colors can be used to mark different denominational affiliations or religious preference (e.g., Presbyterian-blue, New Age-purple, Atheist/secular-black, etc.). If denominational affiliation and religious preference is unknown, then no color is used.

A person who converts to another religious tradition or decides to change denominational affiliations can be depicted by marking in the appropriate color in a circle around the outside of the figure representing the person. The date of the change should also be listed on the genogram beside the symbol in brackets. This provides an indication of the stability or fluidity of affiliation over time (Frame, 2000b).

The line connecting the parents to the children can be color coded based upon the denomination or religious tradition in which the children were raised. Additional colors can be employed if changes occurred during childhood. Building on the above example, a son that was raised in the Islamic tradition until the death of his father at age 10 and was subsequently raised Catholic would have a brown line that changes into a green line running from the parents to the child. The date of the change at age 10 could be recorded on the spiritual genogram at the point where the line changes color from brown to green.

The Limitations of Affiliation

While most clients are affiliated with a particular denomination (Gallup & Lindsay, 1999) and remain in their family of origin's denominational affiliation (O'Connor, et al., 1999; Gallup & Lindsay, 1999), there is growing realization that denominational affiliations are often inaccurate indicators of adherents' beliefs (Clydesdale, 1999). Due to what Hunter (1991) refers to as an epistemologically based religious restructuring, denominational affiliations, and even religious preference to some extent, are growing less significant as indictors of personal spiritual orientation (Hoffmann & Miller, 1998; Sullins, 1999).

As Hunter (1991) observes, many denominations incorporate both orthodox believers, who affirm a transcendent timeless understanding of truth, and progressive adherents, who believe that truth evolves as dictated by the spirit of the present age. Thus, denominations are frequently split to some extent along epistemological lines, with some churches affirming an orthodox or conservative understanding of truth, while others hold a progressive or liberal view. Put differently, due to differences in epistemology, clients can express their spirituality in radically different manners even when members of the same denomination.

As a result of this religious restructuring, epistemology rather than denomination is becoming an increasingly salient marker of one's metaphysical worldview. Due to what Hunter (1991) calls an "ecumenism of orthodoxy," an evangelical United Methodist, a charismatic Episcopalian, and a traditional Catholic may have more in common with each other than members of their own denominations, in spite of significant theological differences that might have hindered such relationships in past generations. Similarly, although to a lesser extent, a devout Hindu, Muslim, or Orthodox Jew may have more in common with a Mormon, due to their shared epistemological approach, than members of their own traditions whose beliefs have been largely secularized by the dominant progressive culture (Fenton, 1988; Smith, 1999; Wuthnow, 1999).

Consequently, an executive who holds an evangelical Christian spiritual orientation might switch denominations with each corporate move, selecting a church with an orthodox understanding of truth. In situations where clients have repeatedly changed denominations, it may be appropriate to discard denominational affiliations entirely when color coding. In addition to depicting the major religious traditions, such as Islam, Buddhism, Hinduism, secularism, etc., color coding might be used to portray the major epistemologically based traditions within Christianity: evangelical Christianity, liberal/mainline Protestantism, and traditional and liberal Roman Catholicism.

Similarly, when working with individuals from other major religious traditions, a similar epistemological demarcation often exists between orthodox believers on the one hand and progressive and secular/cultural adherents on the other. For instance, Fishbane (1999) notes that many individuals now consider the Jewish community to be two separate communities, with the rift so great that Orthodox Jews are unable to sanction their children marrying liberal Jews, who may not be considered Jewish according to traditional rabbinic law.

Integration and Client Selection

It is not uncommon for both denominational and epistemological approaches discussed above to ring true in clients' experience. In such situations, both methods may be incorporated into the genogram by dividing the symbols diagonally in two, with the left half designating the denomination and the right half the epistemological status. For example, while both parents may belong to the same Southern Baptist denomination as their daughter, the client may view her mother as a conservative and her father as a liberal. In this case, the right side of both symbols would be colored red, while the left side of the mother's circle might be colored yellow, to signify conservative beliefs, and the right side of the father's square is colored gray, to indicate liberal beliefs. Similarly, yellow and gray would be used with other individuals in the genogram to indicate orthodox and progressive spiritual orientations, with an additional color being used to depict other orientations if warranted in the client's perception (e.g., pink might be used on the left side of the symbol to portray a nominal, essentially secular Southern Baptist).

It is important to ensure that the religious preference and denominational affiliation accurately represents clients' phenomenological reality. As mentioned above, the essential point of color coding is to reflect the degree of spiritual and religious congruence and dissimilarity that exists throughout the family system. Accordingly, practitioners may wish to explain the basic concepts to clients and allow them to select the colors that most accurately reflect their perceptions in a manner that serves as a good proxy for their spiritual orientation. While religious preference and denominational affiliation provide good starting points, particularly for grandparents, practitioners should seek to move beyond these initial markers to obtain a fuller understanding of how spirituality was expressed in the family system, with clients making the final determinations.

Filling in the Picture

Significant spiritual events should also be recorded on the genogram. Baptisms (water and spirit), confirmations, church memberships, bar and bat mitzvahs, and other events that hold religious import can be included (Frame, 2000b). When possible, symbols drawn from clients' spiritual cosmology should be used to depict these events. For instance, charismatic or pentecostal believers might use a dove to represent the filling of the Holy Spirit while Hindus might draw a relief of a temple to denote the significant effect the opening of a new temple had on their community. In addition to symbols, short summary statements can be delineated on the genogram to note significant events.

Depicting Notable Spiritual Relationships

In addition to depicting religious beliefs, it is also possible to include an affective component as well. Felt spiritual closeness between family members can be illustrated on spiritual genograms. Lines with double-headed arrows can be used to symbolize a relationship in which individuals experience a close reciprocal spiritual bond, with the thickness of the line indicating the intimacy or strength of the relationship (Hodge, 2000a). In situations in which the relationship was more hierarchical and less reciprocal, as might occur with a grandparent mentoring a grandchild, a single arrowhead can be used to depict the flow of spiritual resources. Finally, spiritual conflict can be portrayed with a jagged line, similar to a lightening bolt, drawn between the two individuals.

A Case Example

Diagram 2 (pg. 84) indicates what a relatively straightforward spiritual genogram might look like for a couple, Mark and

Diagram 2

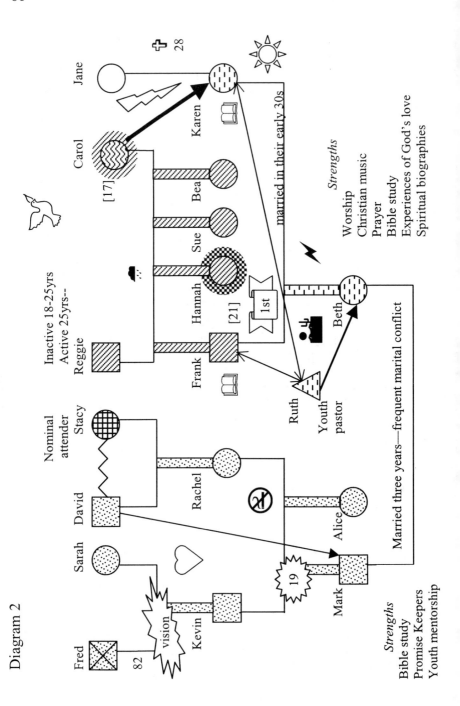

Beth, who are experiencing marital problems. Various patterns (e.g., dots, diagonals, waves, etc.) are employed to depict different denominations in place of the actual colors that would normally be used with a spiritual genogram. As represented by the dotted "color" coding, Mark's family system is characterized by a single denominational affiliation, Southern Baptist, with the exception of his maternal grandmother, Stacy, who was a nominal Methodist. While the shared values have helped the family maintain a relatively close, loving bond, Mark has always felt especially attached to his maternal grandfather, crediting David for helping him to turn his life around in his teens when he was experimenting with illegal substances in defiance of his family's standards. David's mentoring relationship also played an instrumental role in his baptism at age 19, which sparked a full return to active participation in his church . Also noted on Mark's spiritual genogram is that Kevin, Mark's father, had difficulty coming to terms with the death of his 82-year-old father until he received divine comfort in the form of a dream and that David has experienced some spiritual conflict with his wife Stacy over the years.

Beth's family system exhibits a greater degree of spiritual diversity. Her paternal grandmother, Carol, was raised Episcopalian. However, at age 17 she experienced an infilling of the Holy Spirit at an interdenominational Pentecostal youth rally. She subsequently left the Episcopal Church, joining the Assemblies of God, where she met her husband, and raised her four children in that denomination. Although Reggie was only marginally involved in his religious community, his involvement with Carol led to a re-engagement with his church. Hannah, the oldest daughter from Reggie and Carol's marriage, abandoned her faith for agnosticism during her college years, a decision that caused a degree of sorrow in the family.

Beth's parents are both particularly committed Christians, as signified by the open scriptures. Little is known about Beth's maternal grandmother, Jane, and nothing about her maternal grandfather. Beth's mother, Karen, experienced a particularly stormy upbringing that lasted into her mid-20s. A spiritual conversion at 28, and subsequent involvement in the Vineyard Christian Fellowship, led to a significantly sunnier period in Karen's life. As indicated by the heavy line, Carol has played an important role as a mentor in Karen's life after joining the family.

Beth's parents were heavily involved in church activities and have been accorded a number of honors for their contributions. During Beth's late teen years, an international mission trip to work with an oppressed desert dwelling population had a significant influence upon her life, sparking a lifelong sensitivity to social justice issues as she experienced God's heart for the poor and disenfranchised. While Beth has generally gotten along well with her parents, there have been frequent stormy periods, particularly with her mother. Ruth, her youth pastor, has been a significant spiritual influence in her life. Indeed, Ruth is widely respected in her parents' church and has played a role as a spiritual mentor with both of Beth's parents, although the relationship has been reciprocal.

Conducting an Assessment

Given the sacred nature of spirituality for many clients, it is important to obtain clients' consent before exploring the issue. For example, a practitioner might ask Mark and Beth if spirituality feels like an area they wish to explore. Similarly, the spiritual genogram should also be explained and permission secured before initiating construction. The exploration of clients' spiritual cosmologies should be conducted in a spirit of openness and respect which empowers clients to discover their own solutions (Rey, 1997)

Practitioners can safeguard clients' autonomy by monitoring their own and clients' responses to sensitive, value-laden issues to ensure that clients are assenting to the movement of the clinical dialogue. Practitioners should be aware that religious countertransference occurs commonly, particularly when addressing areas in which value systems conflict (Genia, 2000). For instance, feminist practitioners raised in a faith tradition that affirms complementary gender roles, such as Mark's Southern Baptist tradition, may find that clients who hold complementary views on gender relations evoke unresolved emotions that jeopardize the therapeutic relationship (Black, Jeffreys & Hartley, 1993).

Roberts (1999b) suggests that practitioners be sensitive to the biases of the dominant culture toward clients' spiritual belief systems. For instance, the unfounded media-propagated accusations that Muslims were responsible for the Oklahoma City bombing or, alternatively, <u>Time</u> magazine's decision not to mention the Columbine killers were motivated by anti-Christian hatred in their 20-

page cover story reflect prejudice against these two faiths (Rabey, 2000; Roberts, 1999b). Clients may be more receptive toward sharing their personal spiritual narratives if practitioners demonstrate an empathetic awareness of the discrimination people of faith frequently encounter at the hands of the dominant secular culture.

Areas to Explore

While the construction of a spiritual genogram should be as client directed as possible, practitioners play an important role by helping clients explore their spiritual history. To assist in the exploration, practitioners should be aware of a number of common patterns that may exist in clients' histories. While it is critical not to stereotype or generalize regarding spiritual beliefs (Griffith, 1999), it may also be helpful to be aware of some commonly occurring themes that may warrant exploration.

While most individuals are religiously active, over three-quarters become inactive during some point of their lives (O'Connor, et al., 1999). O'Conner and associates (1999) found that the average age at which inactivity began was 21, with the period of inactivity lasting approximately 7 years. Important life decisions that typically occur during the 20s can come back to haunt individuals when they re-engage their spiritual walk later in life. For example, courtship and marriage may occur when either one or both of the parties are inactive in their faith. Conflict may occur when individuals seek to re-connect with their spiritual roots.

Problems may also arise from differing levels of spiritual and religious involvement, even among denominations that hold generally similar theological views. Baptists, for example, may be much more likely to be spiritually and religiously engaged than Methodists or Catholics (O'Connor, et al., 1999). Accordingly, it is important to explore with the client denominational distinctives and how any differences in denomination or religious preference played themselves out in family life.

In aggregate, the salience of spirituality increases with age (Argue, Johnson & White, 1999). Consequently, grandparents may have an added desire to pass on their wisdom to their families, and close, cross-generational spiritual bonds may arise with spiritually receptive grandchildren. Further, in African American, as well as many other minority communities, the role of elders in the transmission of spiritual and religious values may take on a more prominent role (Dancy & Wynn-Dancy, 1994).

Wuthnow (1999) notes that growing up in a devout home places people in a distinct subculture. Much like individuals who fall under Hunter's (1991) ecumenism of orthodoxy, these people are often acutely aware that their values, morals, and perceptions differ from those of the dominant secular culture. As Talbot (2000) observes, in the midst of an ascendant secular culture, these individuals represent the new counterculture. Two prominent indicators that are associated with this discrete outlook are childhood environments in which one's parents read the Bible at home and regularly held family devotions (Wuthnow, 1999).

Major life challenges frequently enhance the personal salience of spirituality (Pargament, 1997). Difficulties often serve to reorient individuals toward an eternal perspective. While crisis can drive people away from God due to perceived lack of help in time of need, they more frequently have the reverse effect, as individuals seek refuge in the only Being that is able to transcend the current crisis (Ferraro & Kelley-Moore, 2000).

Table 3 (see pg. 89) provides practitioners with a list of possible questions that can be used in tandem with the above material to facilitate the exploration and construction of a spiritual genogram. The questions are grouped somewhat thematically, moving toward increasing degrees of personal disclosure. Given the highly personal nature of spirituality for many individuals, clients may find it easier answering questions about relatives' beliefs and practices than their own, at least until a degree of trust has been established. Concurrently, practitioners should not feel locked into any specific order, nor should the exact wording necessarily be retained. Rather, much like the above material, they are offered as a resource to alert practitioners to possible areas of inquiry that can be woven into the therapeutic dialogue to help clients access pertinent data.

Moving Toward Interventions

After the basic historical components of a spiritual genogram are set in place, it is appropriate to shift from the examination and depiction of past dynamics to highlighting present spiritual functioning. The focus shifts from other family members to the client. In this stage of the assessment, practitioners help clients explore how their past spiritual histories have shaped their current spiritual functioning. It also sets the stage for shifting toward interventions.

Table 3

**Possible Questions to Assist in Constructing
a Spiritual Genogram**

What type of religious affiliation characterized each member of your family, going back to your grandparents? How meaningful was their relationship with their denomination/faith? Their church (house of worship)? To what extent were their personal beliefs and those of their church/denomination congruent? What was their level of participation? To what extent did they enjoy religious fellowship? Their spiritual lives?

How did they express their spiritual and religious beliefs? What were the particular rituals or sayings that were commonly evidenced? How were spirituality and religion assets in their lives? How did their spirituality intersect with the difficulties they encountered in life? How did their faith help them cope with trials?

What spiritually significant events (transitions/conversions/changes in affiliations/encounters with transpersonal beings) have occurred in the family? How did these events affect the individuals involved? How did other members react to these changes?

What are the differences (and similarities) among various family members in their beliefs (practices)? How were differences and conflicts managed? Who was the spiritual leader in your family? What role did your grandparents play in your spiritual walk?

What spiritual relationships stand out to you in your childhood years? What are your earliest religious memories? Did your family hold regular devotional times? What types of spiritually-based practices occurred at home? Which members of your family have had most influence on your spiritual walk? Who do you feel closest to in a spiritual sense?

Table 4 (pg. 90) provides a list of sample questions that might be asked to foster reflection on how past history has influenced

Table 4

Questions that Might Be Used for Transitioning to Interventions

In relationship to your family, what are your current religious and spiritual beliefs? How have your beliefs (practices/feelings) changed since childhood (adolescent)? How has your family's beliefs and practices affected your present expression of spirituality?

To what extent do you experience conflict (fellowship/harmony) with other family members over your spiritual beliefs? What have you accepted and rejected from your family's spiritual history? What prompted these decisions?

What sort of patterns do you see emerging over time? How does your present spirituality intersect with these patterns? How has God worked through your family? How has God worked through your family to touch you?

How does your spirituality assist you in dealing with difficulties? Are there religious practices that help you cope with trials? Does the severity of your problem(s) dissipate or disappear when you engage in certain spiritual practices? What does your faith teach about forgiveness? How have you been able to apply this teaching in your own life?

Are there spiritual strengths in your family's history that you could draw upon to help you deal with problems? Are methods of dealing with problems that you might be able to adapt from others? What sort of insights could you draw from your spiritual genogram that might help you to address your current difficulties?

---

present functioning. Keeping in mind the same cautions as noted in regard to Table 3, these questions generally move from personal exploration toward intervention. Consequently, in the context of the ensuing discussion, an attempt should be made to identify spiritual strengths that can be used to address presenting difficulties. Put differently, clients and practitioners should work together to ascertain spiritual resources and how these assets can be brought to bear on problems. As the case example illustrates, insights can be written on the spiritual genogram.

Interventions

While the interventions selected are dependent upon each client's unique life context, and the theoretical orientation of the clinician, there are a number of interventions that flow naturally from a spiritual genogram of which practitioners may wish to be aware. As Stanion, Papadopoulos and Bor (1997) record, constructing and exploring a genogram is a therapeutic intervention that often sparks significant changes. Fresh perspectives and assets that clients had previously been conscious of in only a peripheral sense are brought into concrete relief by their physical depiction. In turn, practitioners can build on these developments to solidify change.

New narratives can often be fostered as clients see themselves as actors in empowering stories. For example, clients may be able to discern God's hand in certain circumstances over the course of time. A pattern of God's personal intervention, previously undiscerned, may be apparent in the genogram. For example, Mark and Beth's spiritual genogram clearly depicts God's intervention in Kevin's life as well as Carol's and Karen's with significant positive ramifications echoing down through the family systems. Instead of seeing themselves as isolated individuals, overwhelmed by life's circumstances, clients see themselves as under the providential care of God. Disempowering discourses can be altered by such insights, opening up new possibilities to address problems (Richert, 1999).

Working with a Christian sample, Pargament and Brant (1998, p. 122) have identified a number of positive attributions that may help individuals cope with crisis. Table 5 (see pg. 92) provides a redacted list of these attributions. Practitioners may be able to foster the adoption of positive narratives by highlighting these attributions when they appear in clients' family histories. Similarly, practitioners may want to explore to what extent these attitudes exist during the construction of spiritual genograms when working with Christian clients.

Cognitive approaches using spiritual content have been demonstrated to be effective with both Muslims (Azhar, Varma & Dharap, 1994; Azhar & Varma, 1995a; Azhar & Varma, 1995b) and

Table 5

Positive Cognitive Attributions during a Crisis
• Thought about how my life is part of a larger physical force
• Worked together with God as partners to get through this hard time
• Looked to God for strength, support, and guidance in this crisis
• Thought about sacrificing my own well-being and living only for God
• Tried to find the lessons from God in the crisis
• Looked for spiritual support from my church in this crisis
• Tried to give spiritual support to others
• Confessed my sins and asked for God's forgiveness
• Asked God to help me find a new purpose in living
Redacted from Pargament and Brant (1998)

Christians (Hawkins, Tan & Turk, 1999; Propst, 1996). Spiritual genograms can be used to detect healthy beliefs that are spiritually based and substitute them for unproductive beliefs in accordance with the standard tenets of cognitive therapy.

Spiritual genograms also afford the opportunity to reconnect with both the spiritual roots and strengths of family members. As Walsh (1999a, p. 43) noted, "restoring vital bonds with a family's religious heritage is healing and empowering." For instance, a young African American struggling with racism might benefit from learning how the Christian beliefs of elderly grandparents enabled them to overcome similar problems (Johnson, 1995). Not only is the relational connection empowering but practical strategies can be gleaned to tackle extant problems. Or to use the case study as an example, Mark may benefit from exploring with his maternal grandfather, David, how to overcome his marital conflicts in light of David's own struggles with his wife. Spiritual genograms may also suggest opportunities to become engaged in local fellowships, church bodies, small groups, and other religious communities. Social support can be a key factor in overcoming problems. For example, Maton and Salem's (1995) longitudinal examination of an evangelical Christian congregation revealed an empowering, supportive, strengths-based atmosphere that engendered an increased sense of self-worth, connectedness, and optimism regarding the future. Additionally, religiously-based social support may be qualitatively and quantitatively superior to social support obtained in other forums (Ellison & George, 1994). In the case of individuals who are not currently involved in a religious group, spiritual genograms may reveal such strengths, perhaps in the lives of other family members, and encourage personal re-engagement with one's own tradition. Alternatively, sporadic attendees may decide to increase their level of interaction. In the case of regular attenders, such as Mark and Beth, the possibility of untapped resources that might be used to address problem areas can be explored.

Rituals can often be used to address problems. The intensity of problems may be attenuated when clients engage in certain rituals, such as prayer, worship, family devotions, scripture reading, music, participation in activities such as Promise Keepers, youth mentoring programs, etc. In solution-based terminology, they often represent a time when "exceptions" from present difficulties are experienced. By building on what works in clients' lives, problems can be overcome in other areas (Kuehl, 1996; Kuehl, 1995). Spiritual genograms can be used to identify current rituals, or those of other family members who have encountered similar problems. For example, a spiritual genogram may reveal a family ritual that fell into disuse after a particular person's death that could be accessed to address a current problem (Roberts, 1999a).

Finally, there is a growing empirical body of work on the efficacy of forgiveness interventions (McCullough, Paragament & Thoresen, 2000). Essentially all major world religions endorse forgiveness as an expression of orthodox faith (Rye, et al., 2000). Spiritual genograms are perhaps the ideal tool to identify conflicted family relationships and tap into the necessary spiritual resources to foster healing. DiBlasio's (1998) article provides a good overview of the use of decision-based forgiveness interventions within the context of intergenerational therapy. It should also be mentioned that many of the practical suggestions DiBlasio lists can be transferred to forgiveness interventions directed toward individuals outside the family unit.

Uses of Spiritual Genograms

Although spiritual genograms can be effective instruments in a number of situations, practitioners may find them to be particularly useful when clients present with problems involving family members or family of origin issues. For example, Heller and Wood's (2000) examination of couples that married individuals from other faiths found that they experienced unique barriers to intimacy that were spiritually based. For these intermarried couples to achieve intimacy levels comparable to those who married within their tradition, the couples had to work through these differences. As the case example illustrates, spiritual genograms serve as an effective tool to expose areas of difference and potential conflict as well as highlighting the respective spiritual strengths each person brings to the relationship.

Conversely, spiritual genograms could also be used with couples from similar backgrounds to increase their level of intimacy. Heller and Wood (2000) found that couples who affirmed the same tradition achieved high intimacy levels based upon their shared understanding. Thus, practitioners may find spiritual genograms to be a useful tool for increasing intimacy by further drawing out similarities and then building upon the couple's commonalties.

Spiritual genograms can also be useful in dealing with recent immigrants from various faith traditions. For instance, Daneshpour (1998) noted that genograms were crucial when working with Muslims due to the sense of cohesion and interdependency among family members. In such cases, spiritual genograms can highlight spiritual resources, important relationships and other spiritually-based information that is significant for understanding clients and ameliorating their problems.

Poole (1998) noted that genograms may be helpful with Hispanics as they show respect for tradition and help connect spiritual and religious dimensions to treatment plans. Similarly, they may also be particularly useful with other populations that have a prominent sense of extended family and/or where spirituality is an important facet of existence, such as African Americans (Frame & Williams, 1996). Conversely, spiritual genograms may be an inappropriate assessment instrument in some situations. For instance, certain clients may not connect past functioning with present conditions and, consequently, may believe that genogram construction constitutes a misuse of therapeutic time (Kuehl, 1995). In such situations, more present focused assessment approaches, such as spiritual ecomaps (see Chapter 4) may better suit clients' desires due to their "here and now" orientation and their relatively rapid construction.

Finally, in light of time limitations, many practitioners are adopting techniques drawn from brief modalities. While a number of interventions profiled in this paper are either drawn from or are congruent with brief approaches, readers interested in further information may wish to consult two articles written by Kuehl (1996; 1995). Kuehl provides an extended discussion on the integration of solution oriented approaches and genograms that can be used to supplement the material presented in this chapter.

Conclusion

The strength of spiritual genograms is their ability to reveal generationally informed spiritual conflicts and resources, and to connect clients with those resources to solve problems. For families and individuals who desire to understand how their religious heritage intersects with present functioning, and draw upon that heritage to address current challenges, this approach may represent the ideal assessment method.

References

Argue, A., Johnson, D. R., & White, L. K. (1999). Age and religiosity: Evidence from a three-wave panel analysis. *Journal for the Scientific Study of Religion, 38*(3), 423-435.

Azhar, M. Z., & Varma, S. L. (1995a). Religious psychotherapy as management of bereavement. *Acta Psychiatrica Scandinavica, 91*, 233-235.

Azhar, M. Z., & Varma, S. L. (1995b). Religious psychotherapy in depressive patients. *Psychotherapy and Psychosomatics, 63,* 165-168.

Azhar, M. Z., Varma, S. L., & Dharap, A. S. (1994). Religious psychotherapy in anxiety disorder patients. *Acta Psychiatrica Scandinavica, 90,* 1-2.

Bart, M. (1998). Spirituality in counseling finding believers. *Counseling Today, 41*(6), 1, 6.

Bengtson, V. L., & Harootyan, R. A. (1994). *Intergenerational linkages.* Washington, DC: Springer Publishing.

Black, P. N., Jeffreys, D., & Hartley, E. K. (1993). Personal history of pscyhosocial trauma in the early life of social work and business students. *Journal of Social Work Education, 29*(2), 171-180.

Bullis, R. K. (1990). Spiritual genograms: Nurturing our spiritual roots. *Church Teachers, 17*(5), 174-175, 190-191.

Bullis, R. K. (1996). *Spirituality in social work practice.* Washington, DC: Taylor & Francis.

Canda, E. R. (1997). Spirituality. In *1997 Supplement.* In R. L. Edwards (Ed.), *Encyclopedia of social work* (19, pp. 299-309). Washington, DC: NASW Press.

Canda, E. R., & Furman, L. D. (1999). *Spiritual diversity in social work practice.* New York: The Free Press.

Carroll, M. M. (1997). Spirituality and clinical social work: Implications of past and current perspectives. *Arete, 62*(1), 25-34.

Clarke, E. J., Preston, M., Raksin, J., & Bengtson, V. L. (1999). Types of conflicts and tensions between older parents and adult children. *The Gerontologist, 39*(3), 261-270.

Clydesdale, T. T. (1999). Toward understanding the role of bible beliefs and higher education in American attitudes toward eradicating poverty, 1964-1996. *Journal for the Scientific Study of Religion, 38*(1), 103-118.

Dancy, J. J., & Wynn-Dancy, M. L. (1994). Faith of our fathers (mothers) living still: Spirituality as a force for the transmission of family values within the black community. *Activities, Adaptation & Aging, 19*(2), 87-105.

Daneshpour, M. (1998). Muslim families and family therapy. *Journal of Marital and*

Family Therapy, 24(3), 355-390.

Davis, N. J., & Robinson, R. V. (1996). Religious orthodoxy in American society: The myth of a monolithic camp. *Journal for the Scientific Study of Religion, 35*(3), 229-245.

DiBlasio, F. A. (1998). The use of a decision-based forgiveness intervention within intergenerational family therapy. *Journal of Family Therapy, 20*(1), 77-94.

Doherty, W. J. (1999). Morality and spirituality in therapy. In F. Walsh (Ed.), *Spiritual resources in family therapy* (pp. 179-192). New York: Gilford Press.

Dor-Shav, N. K., Friedman, B., & Tcherbonogura, R. (1978). Identification, prejudice and aggression. *The Journal of Social Psychology, 104,* 217-222.

Dunn, A. B., & Dawes, S. J. (1999). Spirituality-focused genograms: Keys to uncovering spiritual resources in African American families. *Journal of Multicultural Counseling and Development, 27*(1), 240-254.

Ellison, C. G., & George, L., K. (1994). Religious involvement, social ties, and social support in a Southeastern community. *Journal for the*

Scientific Study of Religion, 33(1), 46-61.

Ellison, C. G., & Levin, J. S. (1998). The religion-health connection: Evidence, theory, and future directions. *Health Education and Behavior, 25*(6), 700-720.

Fenton, J. Y. (1988). *Transplanting religious traditions.* New York: Praeger.

Ferraro, K. F., & Kelley-Moore, J. A. (2000). Religious consolation among men and women: Do health problems spur seeking? *Journal of the Scientific Study of Religion, 39*(2), 220-234.

Fishbane, M. D. (1999). Honor thy father and mother. In F. Walsh (Ed.), *Spiritual resources in family therapy* (pp. 136-156). New York: Guilford Press.

Fitchett, G. (1993). *Assessing spiritual needs.* Minneapolis: Augsburg.

Frame, M. W. (2000a). Constructing religious/spiritual genograms. In R. E. Watts (Ed.), *Techniques in marriage and family counseling.* The family psychology and counseling series, vol. 1. Alexandria, VA: American Counseling Association.

Frame, M. W. (2000b). The spiritual genogram in family

practice. *Journal of Marital and Family Therapy, 26*(2), 211-216.

Frame, M. W., & Williams, C. B. (1996). Counseling African Americans: Integrating spirituality in therapy. *Counseling and Values, 41*(1), 116-28.

Gallup, G. J., & Lindsay, D. M. (1999). *Surveying the religious landscape.* Harrisburg, PA: Morehouse Publishing.

Gartner, J. (1996). Religious commitment, mental health, and prosocial behavior: A review of the empirical literature. In E. P. Shafranske (Ed.), *Religion and the clinical practice of psychology* (pp. 187-214). Washington, DC: American Psychological Association.

Genia, V. (2000). Religious issues in secularly based psychotherapy. *Counseling and Values, 44*(3), 213-221.

Griffith, M. E. (1999). Opening therapy to conversations with a personal God. In F. Walsh (Ed.), *Spiritual resources in family therapy* (pp. 209-222). New York: Guilford Press.

Hardy, K. V., & Laszloffy, T. A. (1995). The cultural genogram: Key to training culturally competent family therapists. *Journal of Marital*

and Family Therapy, 21(3), 227-237.

Hawkins, R. S., Tan, S.-Y., & Turk, A. A. (1999). Secular versus Christian inpatient cognitive-behavioral therapy programs: Impact on depression and spiritual well-being. *Journal of Psychology and 2Theology, 274*(4), 309-318.

Heller, P. E., & Wood, B. (2000). The influence of religious and ethnic differences on martial intimacy: Intermarriage versus intramarriage. *Journal of Marital and Family Therapy, 26*(2), 241-252.

Hodge, D. R. (2000a). Spiritual ecomaps: A new diagrammatic tool for assessing marital and family spirituality. *Journal of Marital and Family Therapy, 26*(1), 229-240.

Hodge, D. R. (2000b). Spirituality: Towards a theoretical framework. *Social Thought, 19*(4), 1-20.

Hoffmann, J. P., & Miller, A. S. (1998). Denominational influences on socially divisive issues: Polarization or continuity? *Journal for the Scientific Study of Religion, 37*(3), 528-546.

Hoyt, M. F. (1998). Introduction. In M. F. Hoyt (Ed.), *The handbook of constructive therapies* (pp. 1-27). San Francisco: Jossey-Bass.

Hunter, J. D. (1991). *Culture Wars*. New York: BasicBooks.

Johnson, C. L. (1995). Determinants of adaptation of oldest old black Americans. *Journal of Aging Studies*, 9(3), 231-244.

Kuehl, B. P. (1996). The use of genograms with solution-based and narrative therapies. *The Family Journal*, 4(1), 5-11.

Kuehl, B. (1995). The solution-oriented genogram: A collaborative approach. *Journal of Marital and Family Therapy*, 21(3), 239-250.

Lewis, K. G. (1989). The use of color-coded genograms in family therapy. *The Journal of Marital and Family Therapy*, 15(2), 169-176.

Lindstrom, T. C. (1995). Experiencing the presence of the dead: Discrepancies in "the sensing experience" and their psychological concomitants. *Omega*, 31(1), 11-21.

Maton, K. I., & Salem, D. A. (1995). Organizational characteristics of empowering community settings: A multiple case study approach. *American Journal of*

Community Practice, 23(5), 631-656.

McCullough, M. E., Paragament, K. I., & Thoresen, C. E. (Editors). (2000). *Forgiveness*. New York: Guilford Press.

McGoldrick, M., Gerson, R., & Shellenberger. (1999). *Genograms: Assessment and intervention* (2). New York: W.W. Norton & Company.

Morse, M., & Perry, P. (1994). *Parting visions*. New York: Villard Books.

O'Connor, T., P., Alexander, E., Hoge, D., Parikh, C., & Grunder, S. (1999, November). Baptist, Catholic, and Methodist teenagers become adults: A 24-year follow-up study of religious behavior and attitudes. Religious Research Association meeting. Boston.

Pargament, K. I. (1997). *The psychology of religion and coping*. New York: Guilford Press.

Pargament, K. I., & Brant, C. R. (1998). Religion and coping. In H. G. Koenig (Ed.), *Handbook of religion and mental health* (pp. 111-128). New York: Academic Press.

Poole, D. L. (1998). Politically correct or culturally competent? *Health and Social Work*, 23(3), 163-166.

Privette, G., Quackenbos, S., & Bundrick, C. M. (1994). Preferences for religious and nonreligious counseling and psychotherapy. *Psychological Reports, 75,* 539-547.

Propst, L. R. (1996). Cognitive-behavioral therapy and the religious person. In E. P. Shafranske (Ed.), *Religion and the clinical practice of psychology* (pp. 391-407). Washington, DC: American Psychological Association.

Rabey, S. (2000, February 7). Videos of hate. *Christianity Today,* p. 21.

Rey, L. D. (1997). Religion as invisible culture: Knowing about and knowing with. *Journal of Family Social Work, 2*(2), 159-177.

Richert, A. J. (1999). Some thoughts on the integration of narrative and humanistic/existential approaches to psychotherapy. *Journal of Psychotherapy Integration, 9*(2), 161-184.

Roberts, J. (1999a). Beyond words: The power of rituals. In F. Walsh (Ed.), *Spiritual resources in family therapy* (pp. 55-78). New York: Guilford Press.

Roberts, J. (1999b). Heart and Soul. In F. Walsh (Ed.), *Spiritual resources in family therapy* (pp. 256-271). New York: Guilford Press.

Rye, M. S., Paragament, K. I., Ali, M. A., Beck, G. L., Dorff, E. N., Hallisey, C., Narayanan, V., & Williams, J. G. (2000). Religious perspectives on forgiveness. In M. E. McCullough, K. I. Paragament & C. E. Thoresen (Eds.), *Forgiveness* (pp. 17-40). New York: Guilford Press.

Sherwood, D. A. (1998). Charitable choice: Opportunity and challenge for Christians in social work. *Social Work and Christianity, 25*(3), 1-23.

Smith, J. I. (1999). *Islam in America.* New York: Columbia University Press.

Spero, M. H. (1990). Parallel dimensions of experience in psychoanalytic psychotherapy of the religious patient. *Psychotherapy, 27*(1), 53-71.

Stanion, P., Papadopoulos, L., & Bor, R. (1997). Genograms in counseling practice: Constructing a genogram (part 2). *Counseling Psychology Quarterly, 10*(2), 139-148.

Sullins, D. P. (1999). Catholic/Protestant trends on abortion: Convergence and polarity. *Journal for the Scientific Study of Religion, 38*(3), 354-369.

Talbot, M. (2000, February 27). A mighty fortress. *The New York Times Magazine*, pp. 34-41, 66-8, 84-5.

Walsh, F. (1999a). Opening family therapy to spirituality. In F. Walsh (Ed.), *Spiritual resources in family therapy* (pp. 28-58). New York: Gilford Press.

Walsh, F. (1999b). Religion and spirituality. In F. Walsh (Ed.), *Spiritual resources in family therapy* (pp. 3-27). New York: Gilford Press.

Wuthnow, R. (1999). *Growing up religious*. Boston: Beacon Press.

CHAPTER SIX

Spiritual Ecograms: An Assessment Instrument for Identifying Clients' Spiritual Strengths in Space and Across Time[7]

Assessment can be understood as the process of gathering and organizing data into a coherent format that provides the basis for interventions (Rauch, 1993). As Hartman (1995) observes, information exists through time as well as in present life space. In addition to being immersed in a network of existential relationships in the here-and-now, each individual is also part of a family story that stretches across a number of generations.

These intergenerational linkages frequently form an integral component of an individual's spiritual journey. Each generation tends to shape the spiritual beliefs and practices of successive generations (Wuthnow, 1999). To depict this historical influence across time, spiritual genograms are commonly used (Bullis, 1990; Hodge, 2001; Rey, 1997; Roberts, 1999b).

Concurrently, an array of spiritual assets frequently exists in people's present ecological environments. Individuals draw from strengths that exist in life space to help them overcome current obstacles. Spiritual ecomaps, or ecological maps, can be used to portray these extant spiritual strengths in diagrammatic format (Hodge, 2000; Hodge & Williams, in press).

Ideally, assessment should include both time and space dimensions. Accordingly, this chapter presents the spiritual ecogram, which integrates both dimensions in a single pen-and-paper assessment tool. The mechanics of constructing a spiritual ecogram are profiled first and illustrated with a case example. Information is then presented on steps that can be taken to conduct a spiritually competent assessment followed by a discussion of

---

[7] Much of the material in this chapter will be appearing in an upcoming issue of *Families in Society* in an article written by D. R. Hodge entitled, "Spiritual Ecograms: A New Assessment Instrument for Identifying Clients' Spiritual Strengths in Space and Across Time" (in press). This material is used in this book with the permission of *Families in Society*.

spiritual interventions that flow from an ecogram. The chapter concludes with a brief discussion of the advantages of, and alternatives to, spiritual ecograms.

Constructing a Spiritual Ecogram

Constructing spiritual ecograms is similar to fabricating traditional genograms and ecomaps. The client is drawn in the center of the paper. By convention, a circle commonly represents a female and a square depicts a male. Working up from the client, the top half of the page is used to chart a family tree and associated social data. Typically, the basic family structure over three generations is delineated in keeping with standard genogram conventions (McGoldrick, Gerson & Shellenberger, 1999; Stanion, Papadopoulos & Bor, 1997).

While the top half of the page depicts the client's spiritual history through time, the bottom half of the page emphasizes the client's spirituality in space. Consistent with standard ecomap conventions (Hartman, 1995), this portion of the ecogram is used to portray the client's extant relationships with spiritual systems. Important spiritual systems, such as God, rituals, and faith communities, are represented as circles on the outskirts of the paper in a radius around the client (Hodge, 2000; Hodge & Williams, in press). The names of the respective systems are written inside of the circles or domains.

A Case Example

Diagram 3 (see pg. 104) provides an idea of what one person's ecogram might look like. The father's side of Karen's family is characterized by Roman Catholic affiliation. Similarly, with the exception of her maternal grandmother who left her Methodist affiliation for Catholicism at age 21 when she married her husband, the other side is also Catholic. Karen's mother, Kate, died at age 52. Kate experienced a dramatic outpouring of God's love in her early thirties, which is denoted by the heart and the dove representing the work of the Holy Spirit. As a result of this outpouring, at age 35, Kate left her more traditional Catholic church and started going to a charismatic Catholic church that emphasized the work of the Holy Spirit. Karen's brother, Karl, had a spiritual awakening at an interdenominational summer camp at age 14, which eventually led him into a Calvary Chapel fellowship.

Diagram 3

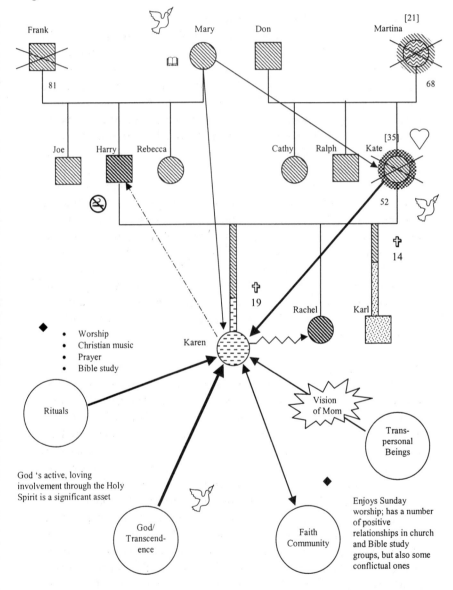

While Karen's father, Harry, and her sister, Rachel, are not particularly devout, they are both firm believers in the importance of remaining in the Catholic fold. This has led to some tension between them and Karen, who experienced a spiritual awakening of her own at age 19 and is now a member of the Assemblies of God. Karen feels that her father tends toward legalism and finds interaction with him to be somewhat of a strain due in part to repeated suggestions that she should return to her Catholic roots. The tension is a little stronger with her sister, Rachel, who, seeing both her siblings leave the fold, feels a particular obligation to maintain the family's Catholic identity.

In contrast to her relationship with her father, Karen's relationship with her mother was quite positive, particularly after Karen's spiritual awakening. Karen's paternal grandmother has also been a significant source of strength to both Karen and her mother. As signified by the open Bible and the presence of the dove, Mary was a particularly committed Christian who allowed the Holy Spirit to operate deeply in her life.

When Karen's mother died, Mary was a particular source of encouragement, as was a vision she received from God assuring her of her mother's well-being in heaven. Karen also feels that angels have intervened in her life on a regular basis.

The most important strength in Karen's life, represented by the heavy line, is her relationship with Jesus. As is the case with her mother and paternal grandmother, the dove symbolizes a deep work of the Holy Spirit, who has progressively deepened her level of intimacy with Jesus. God is perceived as being personally involved with her life and actively working through various events with Karen's best interest at heart.

Rituals that nurture this relationship are also a significant asset. Music that helps her to focus on her relationship with God is an especially rich source of strength. While Bible study and prayer are important, Christian music and worship help her to regain perspective and reorder her priorities when she becomes overwhelmed with life's obstacles.

Karen's relationship with her faith community is more mixed. Her involvement in Bible study and other church functions are generally perceived to be a source of strength, particularly the Sunday morning worship service. Concurrently, there are a number of individuals in her church body that function as a drain on her emotional batteries.

Steps toward Spiritually Competent Assessment

Perhaps the first step toward conducting spiritually competent assessments is undertaking a spiritual self-assessment (Fitchett & Handzo, 1998). In other words, practitioners should seek to understand their own spiritual beliefs and formative religious experiences. By developing their understanding of their own spiritual beliefs, and how they differ from those of various client populations, practitioners are better equipped to facilitate a safe, respectful environment.

In addition to coming to terms with their own spiritual worldview, practitioners should also develop an understanding of the spiritual worldviews their clients commonly affirm. Respecting clients' spiritual autonomy is difficult, if not impossible, if practitioners have little understanding of clients' beliefs and values. As is the case with other areas of diversity, helping professionals should seek to achieve an empathetic, strengths based understanding that allows the practitioner to see reality through the eyes of others.

This understanding should extend to developing an awareness of the bias that people of faith encounter in the dominant secular culture (Roberts, 1999b). For instance, popular media delegitimizes devout Christians and other people of faith by either eliminating them from popular culture or framing them in a negative light (Lindsey & Heeren, 1992; Perkins, 1984; Skill & Robinson, 1994; Skill, Robinson, Lyons & Larson, 1994). Clients are likely to be more willing to share their spiritual narratives if practitioners demonstrate understanding and sensitivity regarding the discrimination committed believers often encounter in the dominant culture. As is common practice, learning about various worldviews by exposing oneself to material written by individuals who affirm the worldview themselves is critical. Reading material on religious worldviews written by members of the dominant secular culture may be counterproductive as such material tends to reflect the biases associated with dominant cultural status (Hodge, Baughman & Cummings, 2002).

As an expression of respect for clients' spiritual autonomy, it is appropriate to secure consent before conducting a spiritual assessment. After establishing rapport with the client, the importance of spirituality can be affirmed followed by an invitation to explore the subject (Maugans, 1996). For example, a practitioner might say, "For many people, spirituality is an important strength. Consequently, I was wondering if you would be interested in exploring how spiritual strengths might be used to address some of the problems you have mentioned." If the client expresses an interest, the ecogram can be explained, and if the client agrees, a personalized ecogram can be constructed.

As implied above, during assessment the focus should not be on determining whether clients' spiritual beliefs are right or wrong, but rather on how their values assist them in coping with difficulties. The practitioner's job is not to accept or reject clients' spiritual values but to help them use their beliefs and practices to assist clients in overcoming their problems (Fitchett & Handzo, 1998).

In some cases, however, practitioners may feel that clients' spiritual beliefs are unproductive. In such situations, practitioners should not attempt to change clients' values in an area that lies outside the realm of their professional competence. Rather, practitioners should collaborate with or refer such clients to clergy (Johnson, Ridley & Nielsen, 2000). Given that this is clergy's area of professional competency, pastors, priests, and other spiritual specialists are better equipped to ascertain the appropriateness of a given set of beliefs and practices. It is critical, however, that practitioners respect clients' spiritual autonomy by forming collaborations with clergy that share the same denominational and theological orientation as the client.

Interventions that Flow from Ecograms

As noted in the introduction, assessment consists of more than just gathering information about a client's spiritual history and strengths on an ecogram. The point of delineating this material is to ascertain the existence of spiritual resources that can be used to solve problems. A critical component of assessment is working together with clients to decide how their spiritual assets might be used to address various challenges they face.

Reviewed immediately below are a number of empirically validated spiritual interventions. Contingent upon the practitioner's theoretical orientation and the unique life context of the client, practitioners can explore their utility with clients. Yet, to reiterate a central point of the preceding section, practitioners should attempt to explore interventions that are congruent with clients' spiritual beliefs and values. Also notable, is the fact that the interventions discussed below can be understood to flow from ecograms. Consequently, when gathering information, it may be useful to bear in mind these interventions in order to better integrate this information into the assessment process.

Ecograms can be used to foster the adoption of new narratives. A series of difficulties can result in the formation of disempowering narratives (Richert, 1999). Clients feel trapped, overwhelmed by problems, with little hope of overcoming their present circumstances. Ecograms can help promote empowering narratives in at least two ways.

First, the physical depiction of clients' subjective strengths can help bring their assets into focus, enhancing their salience through concrete depiction (Moon, 1994). As clients actually see themselves surrounded by strengths, they tend to envision themselves differently, as people with resources and capabilities (Saleebey, 2000). To follow up on the case example, while Karen may be overwhelmed with her problems, seeing her strengths physically depicted can help foster the adoption of a more strength-based self-narrative.

Second, ecograms can help alleviate the sense of hopelessness and purposelessness in which problems flourish. Spirituality tends to engender hope, purpose and meaning. Thus, in addition to highlighting clients' strengths, the specific set of strengths that are elicited tend to shrink the existential concerns that underlie many problems (Lantz, 1998). Practitioners can help clients adopt new narratives by accenting pertinent aspects of clients' spiritual worldviews (Pargament, 1997). With Karen, for example, a practitioner might explore the sense of hope and purpose her Christian belief system fosters.

Encouraging clients to develop their spiritual life can be an effective intervention (Kisthardt, 1997). Strengths in one area may naturally be leveraged to address obstacles in other areas (Sullivan, 1997). For example, a prospective study of clients in India wrestling with schizophrenia (N = 386) found that increased religiousness was related to better outcomes at the two-year follow-up point (Verghese et al., 1989). Conversely, clients who reported a decrease in their religious activities experienced deteriorating health outcomes.

Additionally, a number of studies have found that spiritual practices can ameliorate problems. Spiritual mourning, a ritual characterized by praying, fasting, and seeking God, has been shown to alleviate psychological distress (Griffith, Mahy & Young, 1986). Spiritual pilgrimages have been associated with reduced levels of anxiety and depression (Morris, 1982). Prayer has been shown to enhance the recovery of hospitalized patients (Byrd, 1988). Similarly, various forms of meditation have been associated with well-being (Ellison, 1993; Keefe, 1996). Christian devotional meditation has been associated with reduced levels of stress (Carlson, Bacaseta & Simanton, 1988). Vipassana Buddhist meditation has been demonstrated to reduce ego-defense mechanisms (Emavardhana & Tori, 1997). In short, spiritual practices drawn from clients' frames of reference can be explored as a means of addressing these and possibly other life challenges. In Karen's situation, the practitioner might explore the possibility of Biblically-based devotional meditations on therapeutically beneficial scripture passages.

Rituals can also be interfaced with solution-focused approaches (Kuehl, 1995, 1996). For instance, rituals often represent times when "exceptions" from difficulties are experienced. In addition to identifying current rituals, ecograms might be used to identify traditional family rituals that have fallen into disuse that might be used to address problems (Roberts, 1999a). For instance, in Karen's case, the practitioner might explore the use of worship music as a possible time when exceptions to the problem occur.

Ecograms can be used to elicit health pro-motive beliefs for use in spiritually based cognitive therapy. In this form of therapy, spiritual beliefs that are congruent with the precepts of cognitive therapy are integrated into standard therapeutic techniques. In other words, salutary tenets from the client's spiritual worldview, which hold an added measure of significance to the client, are incorporated into traditional forms of cognitive therapy. Albert Ellis (2000), widely considered to be one the founders of cognitive therapy, has translated a number of his precepts into theistic language in a recent article. Similarly, Backus (1985) provides a book length treatment of the subject that may be particularly helpful when working with Christian clients.

One belief that is widely shared by many faith traditions is the importance of forgiveness (McCullough, Weaver, Larson &

Aay, 2000). A growing body of work on forgiveness in clinical settings exists (McCullough et al., 2000). In addition to delineating spiritual assets that might be used to facilitate forgiveness, ecograms can be used to chart relationships where forgiveness is needed. An article length discussion of decision-based forgiveness interventions is provided by DiBlasio (1998).

Ecograms can also reveal the existence of therapeutically beneficial mentoring relationships. Karen, for example, reports that her relationship with Mary is a source of strength. Consequently, the practitioner might explore whether interacting with Mary on a more regular basis might help Karen alleviate her difficulties.

Finally, ecograms may suggest practitioners explore the potentialities that exist for clients in local fellowships, church bodies, small groups, and other religious communities. In addition to offering a wide array of services, church groups and other faith-based or religious fellowships often foster an enhanced sense of psychological resources, control over life's circumstances, life direction, and social support (Ellison & George, 1994; Haight, 1998; Maton & Salem, 1995). Practitioners can explore opportunities for further involvement, such as the existence of programs and support groups or even opportunities to start new programs that directly address the issues clients are struggling with.

Advantages of and Alternatives to Ecograms

Ecograms offer essentially all the assessment advantages offered by traditional spiritual ecomaps and genograms. In addition, however, ecograms allow practitioners and clients to see the connections between past and present functioning. Historical influences on current systems can be seen and present relationships with historical influences can also be seen on an ecogram.

The ability to depict these connections is a unique feature of ecograms. Consequently, ecograms may allow clients to see relationships in a manner that offers fresh insights into their current situation. Resources associated with the past may take on new meaning when individuals see their connection to their present reality.

Nevertheless, in some situations, it may be advisable to use alternative assessment approaches. For example, some clients may feel that the exploration of the past has little to do with present problems, (Kuehl 1995). For such individuals, assessment approaches with focus on present functioning, such as traditional spiritual ecomaps (Hodge, 2000; Hodge & Williams, in press) may better suit clients' needs. Conversely, spiritual genograms may be more appropriate in contexts that involve just the immediate family system, such as a couple attempting to work through differing spiritual traditions.

Ecograms were developed specifically for spiritual assessment. However, they can also be adapted for use with individuals for whom spirituality is a less salient concern. This is accomplished by using traditional ecomap systems (Hartman, 1995), such as work, recreation, and school, in place of the spiritual systems. Alternatively, spirituality could be incorporated as one system alongside the other traditional systems. This allows practitioners to conduct a holistic assessment that incorporates information across time and in space on a single diagrammatic instrument. As implied above, the ability to depict the connections between time and space dimensions is an important assessment asset that practitioners may desire to utilize in general assessment.

References

Argue, A., Johnson, D. R., & White, L. K. (1999). Age and religiosity: Evidence from a three-wave panel analysis. *Journal for the Scientific Study of Religion, 38*(3), 423-435.

Azhar, M. Z., & Varma, S. L. (1995a). Religious psychotherapy as management of bereavement. *Acta Psychiatrica Scandinavica, 91,* 233-235.

Azhar, M. Z., & Varma, S. L. (1995b). Religious psychotherapy in depressive patients. *Psychotherapy and Psychosomatics, 63,* 165-168.

Azhar, M. Z., Varma, S. L., & Dharap, A. S. (1994). Religious psychotherapy in anxiety disorder patients. *Acta Psychiatrica Scandinavica, 90,* 1-2.

Babchuk, N., & Whitt, H. P. (1990). R-order and religious switching. *Journal of the Scientific Study of Religion, 29,* 246-254.

Backus, W. (1985). *Telling the truth to troubled people.* Minneapolis: Bethany House.

Bengtson, V. L., & Harootyan, R. A. (1994). *Intergenerational linkages.* Washington, DC: Springer Publishing.

Bullis, R. K. (1990). Spiritual genograms: Nurturing our spiritual roots. *Church*

Teachers, 17(5), 174-175, 190-191.

Bullis, R. K. (1996). Spirituality in social work practice. Washington, DC: Taylor & Francis.

Byrd, R. C. (1988). Positive therapeutic effects of intercessory prayer in a coronary care unit population. Southern Medical Journal, 81(7), 826-829.

Canda, E. R. (1997). Spirituality. In R. L. Edwards (Ed.), Encyclopedia of social work (19th ed., pp. 299-309). Washington, DC: NASW Press.

Canda, E. R., & Furman, L. D. (1999). Spiritual diversity in social work practice. New York: The Free Press.

Carlson, C. R., Bacaseta, P. E., & Simanton, D. A. (1988). A controlled evaluation of devotional meditation and progressive relaxation. Journal of Psychology and Theology, 14(4), 362-368.

Carroll, M. M. (1997). Spirituality and clinical social work: Implications of past and current perspectives. Arete, 22(1), 25-34.

Clarke, E. J., Preston, M., Raksin, J., & Bengtson, V. L. (1999). Types of conflicts and tensions between older parents and adult children.

The Gerontologist, 39(3), 261-270.

Cowger, C. D. (1994). Assessing client strengths: Clinical assessments for client empowerment. Social Work, 39(3), 262-268.

Derezotes, D. S. (1995). Spirituality and religiosity: Neglected factors in social work practice. Arete, 20(1), 1-15.

DiBlasio, F. A. (1998). The use of a decision-based forgiveness intervention within intergenerational family therapy. Journal of Family Therapy, 20(1), 77-94.

Ellis, A. (2000). Can rational emotive behavior therapy be effectively used with people who have devout beliefs in God and religion? Professional Psychology: Research and Practice, 31(1), 29-33.

Ellison, C. G. (1993). Religious involvement and self-perception among Black Americans. Social Forces, 71(4), 1027-1055.

Ellison, C. G., & George, L., K. (1994). Religious involvement, social ties, and social support in a Southeastern community. Journal for the Scientific Study of Religion, 33(1), 46-61.

Ellison, C. G., & Levin, J. S. (1998). The religion-health connection: Evidence, theory, and future directions. *Health Education and Behavior, 25*(6), 700-720.

Emavardhana, T., & Tori, C. D. (1997). Changes in self-concept, ego defense mechanisms, and religiosity following seven-day Vipassana meditation retreats. *Journal for the Scientific Study of Religion, 36*(2), 194-206.

Ferraro, K. F., & Kelley-Moore, J. A. (2000). Religious consolation among men and women: Do health problems spur seeking? *Journal of the Scientific Study of Religion, 39*(2), 220-234.

Fitchett, G. (1993). *Assessing spiritual needs*. Minneapolis: Augsburg.

Fitchett, G., & Handzo, G. (1998). Spiritual assessment, screening, and intervention. In J. C. Holland (Ed.), *Psycho-oncology* (pp. 790-808). New York: Oxford University Press.

Furman, L. D., Perry, D., & Goldale, T. (1996). Interaction of Evangelical Christians and social workers in the rural environment. *Human Services in the Rural Environment, 19*(3), 5-8.

Gallup, G. J., & Castelli, J. (1989). *The people's religion: American faith in the 90's*. New York: Macmillan.

Genia, V. (2000). Religious issues in secularly based psychotherapy. *Counseling and Values, 44*(3), 213-221.

Gilbert, M. (2000). Spirituality in social work groups: Practitioners speak out. *Social Work with Groups, 22*(4), 67-84.

Griffith, E. E., Mahy, G. E., & Young, J. L. (1986). Psychological benefits of Spiritual Baptist "mourning": II. An empirical assessment. *Amer-ican Journal of Psychiatry, 143*(2), 226-229.

Griffith, M. E. (1999). Opening therapy to conversations with a personal God. In F. Walsh (Ed.), *Spiritual resources in family therapy* (pp. 209-222). New York: Guilford Press.

Haight, W. L. (1998). "Gathering the spirit" at first Baptist church: Spirituality as a protective factor in the lives of African American children. *Social Work, 43*(3), 213-221.

Hardy, K. V., & Laszloffy, T. A. (1995). The cultural genogram: Key to training culturally competent family therapists. *Journal of Marital and Family Therapy, 21*(3), 227-237.

Hartman, A. (1995). Diagrammatic assessment of family relationships. *Families in Society, 76*(2), 111-122.

Hawkins, R. S., Tan, S.-Y., & Turk, A. A. (1999). Secular versus Christian inpatient cognitive-behavioral therapy programs: Impact on depression and spiritual well-being. *Journal of Psychology and Theology, 274*(4), 309-318.

Hodge, D. R. (2000). Spiritual ecomaps: A new diagrammatic tool for assessing marital and family spirituality. *Journal of Marital and Family Therapy, 26*(1), 229-240.

Hodge, D. R. (2001). Spiritual genograms: A generational approach to assessing spirituality. *Families in Society, 82*(1), 35-48.

Hodge, D. R., Baughman, L. M., & Cummings, J. A. (2002, February 24-27). *Moving toward spiritual competency: Deconstructing religious stereotypes and spiritual prejudices in social work literature.* Paper presented at the [Forty-eighth annual program meeting] Council on Social Work Education. Nashville, TN.

Hodge, D. R., & Williams, T. R. (In press). Assessing African American spirituality with spiritual eco-maps. *Families in Society.*

Hwang, S.-C., & Cowger, C., D. (1998). Utilizing strengths in assessment. *Families in Society, 79*(1), 25-31.

Jacobs, J. L. (1992). Religious ritual and mental health. In J. Schumaker (Ed.), *Religion and mental health* (pp. 291-299). New York: Oxford University Press.

Jensen, J. P., & Bergin, A. E. (1988). Mental health values of professional therapists: A national interdisciplinary survey. *Professional Psychology: Research and Practice, 19*(3), 290-297.

Johnson, W. B., Ridley, C. R., & Nielsen, S. L. (2000). Religiously sensitive rational emotive behavior therapy: Elegant solutions and ethical risks. *Professional Psychology: Research and Practice, 31*(1), 14-20.

Kark, J. D., Shemi, G., Friedlander, Y., Martin, O., Manor, O., & Blondheim, S. H. (1996). Does religious observance promote health? Mortality in secular vs. religious kibbutzim in Israel. *American Journal of Public Health, 86*(3), 341-346.

Keefe, T. (1996). Meditation and social work treatment. In F. Turner (Ed.), *Social work treatment* (pp. 434-460). New York: The Free Press.

Kisthardt, W. (1997). The strengths model of case management: Principles and helping functions. In D. Saleebey (Ed.), *The strengths perspective in social work practice* (pp. 97-113). White Plains, NY: Longman.

Koenig, H. G. (1998). Religious attitudes and practices of hospitalized medically ill older adults. *International Journal of Geriatric Psychiatry, 13,* 213-224.

Koenig, H. G., McCullough, M. E., & Larson, D. B. (2001). *Handbook of religion and health.* New York: Oxford University Press.

Kuehl, B. P. (1995). The solution-oriented genogram: A collaborative approach. *Journal of Marital and Family Therapy, 21*(3), 239-250.

Kuehl, B. P. (1996). The use of genograms with solution-based and narrative therapies. *The Family Journal, 4*(1), 5-11.

Lantz, J. (1998). Recollection in existential psychotherapy with older adults. *Journal of Clinical Geropsychology, 4*(1), 45-53.

Lindsey, D. B., & Heeren, J. (1992). Where the sacred meets the profane: Religion in the comic pages. *Review of Religious Research, 34*(1), 63-77.

Lindstrom, T. C. (1995). Experiencing the presence of the dead: Discrepancies in "the sensing experience" and their psychological concomitants. *Omega, 31*(1), 11-21.

Maton, K. I., & Salem, D. A. (1995). Organizational characteristics of empowering community settings: A multiple case study approach. *American Journal of Community Practice, 23*(5), 631-656.

Mattaini, M. A., & Kirk, S. A. (1991). Assessing assessment in social work. *Social Work, 36*(3), 260-266.

Maugans, T. A. (1996). The spiritual history. *Archives of Family Medicine, 5*(1), 11-16.

McCullough, M. E., Weaver, A. J., Larson, D. B., & Aay, K. R. (2000). Psychotherapy with mainline Protestants: Lutheran, Presbyterian, Episcopal/Anglican, and Methodist. In P. S. Richards & A. E. Bergin (Eds.), *Handbook of psychotherapy and religious diversity* (pp. 105-129). Washington, DC: American Psychological Association.

McGoldrick, M., Gerson, R., & Shellenberger. (1999). *Genograms: Assessment and intervention* (2nd ed.). New York: W.W. Norton & Company.

Moon, B. L. (1994). *Introduction to art therapy.* Springfield, IL: Charles C Thomas.

Morris, P. A. (1982, May). The effects of pilgrimage on anxiety, depression and religious attitude. *Psychological Medicine, 12*(2), 291-294.

Morse, M., & Perry, P. (1994). *Parting visions.* New York: Villard Books.

O'Connor, T., P., Alexander, E., Hoge, D., Parikh, C., & Grunder, S. (1999, November). *Baptist, Catholic, and Methodist teenagers become adults: A 24-year follow-up study of religious behavior and attitudes.* Paper Presented at the Meeting of the Religious Research Association, Boston, MA.

Pargament, K. I. (1997). *The psychology of religion and coping.* New York: Guilford Press.

Patterson, J., Hayworth, M., Turner, C., & Raskin, M. (2000). Spiritual issues in family therapy: A graduate-level course. *Journal of Martial and Family Therapy, 26*(2), 199-210.

Perkins, H. W. (1984). Religious content in American, British, and Canadian popular publications from 1937 to 1979. *Sociological Analysis, 45*(2), 159-165.

Perry, B. G. F. (1998). The relationship between faith and well-being. *Journal of Religion and Health, 37*(2), 125-136.

Propst, L. R. (1996). Cognitive-behavioral therapy and the religious person. In E. P. Shafranske (Ed.), *Religion and the clinical practice of psychology* (pp. 391-407). Washington, DC: American Psychological Association.

Rauch, J. B. (1993). *Assessment: A sourcebook for social work practice.* Milwaukee: Families International.

Rey, L. D. (1997). Religion as invisible culture: Knowing about and knowing with. *Journal of Family Social Work, 2*(2), 159-177.

Richards, P. S., & Bergin, A. E. (Eds.). (2000). *Handbook of psychotherapy and religious diversity.* Washington, DC: American Psychological Association.

Richards, P. S., Owen, L., & Stein, S. (1993). A religiously oriented group counseling intervention for self-defeating perfectionism: A pilot study. *Counseling and Values, 37,* 96-104.

Richert, A. J. (1999). Some thoughts on the integration of narrative and humanistic/existential approaches to psychotherapy. *Journal of Psychotherapy Integration, 9*(2), 161-184.

Roberts, J. (1999a). Beyond words: The power of rituals. In F. Walsh (Ed.), *Spiritual resources in family therapy* (pp. 55-78). New York: Guilford Press.

Roberts, J. (1999b). Heart and Soul. In F. Walsh (Ed.), *Spiritual resources in family therapy* (pp. 256-271). New York: Guilford Press.

Ronnau, J., & Poertner, J. (1993). Identification and use of strengths: A family system approach. *Children Today, 22*(2), 20-23.

Saleebey, D. (2000). Power in the people: Strengths and hope. *Advances in Social Work, 1*(2), 127-136.

Sheridan, M. J., & Amato-von Hemert, K. (1999). The role of religion and spirituality in social work education and practice: A survey of student views and experiences. *Journal of Social Work Education, 35*(1), 125-141.

Sheridan, M. J., Bullis, R. K., Adcock, C. R., Berlin, S. D., & Miller, P. C. (1992). Practitioners' personal and professional attitudes and behaviors toward religion and spirituality: Issues for education and practice. *Journal of Social Work Education, 28*(2), 190-203.

Sheridan, M. J., Wilmer, C. M., & Atcheson, L. (1994). Inclusion of content on religion and spirituality in the social work curriculum: A study of faculty views. *Journal of Social Work Education, 30*(3), 363-376.

Sherwood, D. A. (1998). Spiritual assessment as a normal part of social work practice: Power to help and power to harm. *Social Work & Christianity, 25*(2), 80-100.

Skill, T., & Robinson, J. D. (1994). The image of Christian leaders in fictional television programs. *Sociology of Religion, 55*(1), 75-84.

Skill, T., Robinson, J. D., Lyons, J. S., & Larson, D. (1994). The portrayal of religion and spirituality on fictional network television. *Review of the Religious Research, 35*(3), 251-267.

Stanion, P., Papadopoulos, L., & Bor, R. (1997). Genograms in counseling practice: Constructing a genogram (part 2). *Counseling Psychology Quarterly, 10*(2), 139-148.

Sullivan, W. P. (1997). On strengths, niches, and recovery from serious mental illness. In D. Saleebey (Ed.), *The strengths perspective in social work practice* (pp. 183-199). White Plains, NY: Longman.

Verghese, A., John, J. K., Rajkumar, S., Richard, J., Sethi, B. B., & Trivedi, J. K. (1989). Factors associated with the course and outcome of schizophrenia in India: Results of a two-year multicentre follow-up study. *British Journal of Psychiatry, 154,* 499-503.

Worthington, E. J., Kurusu, T., McCullough, M., & Sandage, S. (1996). Empirical research on religion and psychotherapeutic processes and outcomes: A 10-year review and research prospectus. *Psychological Bulletin, 119*(3), 448-487.

Wuthnow, R. (1999). *Growing up religious.* Boston: Beacon Press.

CHAPTER SEVEN

Conclusion

This handbook has collected in one location five complementary assessment tools, verbally based spiritual histories, spiritual lifemaps, spiritual ecomaps, spiritual genograms and spiritual ecograms. Each assessment tool has unique strengths and advantages that suggest its use with various clients and particular contexts.

Regardless of which spiritual assessment instrument is used, it is critical that helping professionals consider and develop spiritual competency. It is perhaps helpful to envision spirituality competency in the form of a continuum ranging from spiritually destructive practice on one end through to spiritually competent practice on the other end (Manoleas, 1994). Developing spiritual competency is a life-long process — no one has fully arrived. Practitioners are commonly at different places along the continuum with different spiritual groups. For example, a practitioner may be relatively more competent working with clients' from liberal Protestant traditions than clients from Islamic traditions.

The goal of spiritual competency is fourfold: (1) to become aware of the cognitive grid, worldview, or lens used to see faith-based cultures: (2) to learn how the biases associated with one's own lens affects one's understanding of people from that particular faith group; (3) to learn to set aside the lens and associated biases and see reality through the worldview used by the faith group; and (4) to come to a point of appreciating reality as seen through the eyes of the client's worldview.

Helping professionals who work with clients from particular faith traditions on a consistent basis might consider becoming familiar with the norms of those faith traditions. This process can assist in understanding better the worldview of clients from a given faith tradition as well as how one's own worldview differs from the clients'.

The following citations refer to articles and book chapters about various faith traditions that readers may find helpful. In other words, these works can serve as starting points for further research on understanding such groups as evangelical Christians (DiBlasio, 1988), Pentecostals (Dobbins, 2000), Catholics (Shafranske, 2000), mainline Protestants (McCullough, Weaver, Larson & Aay, 2000), Mormons (Ulrich, Richards & Bergin, 2000), Muslims (Daneshpour, 1998), Judaism (Zedek, 1998), Native American spirituality (Trujillo, 2000), Hinduism (Juthani, 1998) and Buddhism (Scotton, 1998). Readers may also wish to consider the text by Van Hook, Hugen and Aguilar (2001), which also provides insights into a number of different faith traditions. By gleaning knowledge from these and other sources, helping professionals will be better equipped to conduct spiritually competent assessments.

References

Daneshpour, M. (1998). Muslim families and family therapy. *Journal of Marital and Family Therapy, 24*(3), 355-390.

DiBlasio, F. A. (1988). Integrative strategies for family therapy with Evangelical Christians. *Journal of Psychology and Theology, 16*(2), 127-134.

Dobbins, R. D. (2000). Psychotherapy with Pentecostal Protestants. In P. S. Richards & A. E. Bergin (Eds.), *Handbook of psychotherapy and religious diversity* (pp. 155-184). Washington, DC: American Psychological Association.

Juthani, N. V. (1998). Understanding and treading Hindu patients. In H. G. Koenig (Ed.), *Handbook of religion and mental health*

(pp. 271-278). New York: Academic Press.

Manoleas, P. (1994). An outcome approach to assessing the cultural competence of MSW students. *Journal of Multicultural Social Work, 3*(1), 43-57.

McCullough, M. E., Weaver, A. J., Larson, D. B., & Aay, K. R. (2000). Psychotherapy with mainline Protestants: Lutheran, Presbyterian, Episcopal/Anglican, and Methodist. In P. S. Richards & A. E. Bergin (Eds.), *Handbook of psychotherapy and religious diversity* (pp. 105-129). Washington, DC: American Psychological Association.

Scotton, B. W. (1998). Treating Buddhist patients. In H. G. Koenig (Ed.), *Handbook of religion and mental health* (pp. 263-270). New York: Academic Press.

Shafranske, E. P. (2000). Psychotherapy with Roman Catholics. In P. S. Richards & A. E. Bergin (Eds.), *Handbook of psychotherapy and religious diversity* (pp. 59-88). Washington, DC: American Psychological Association.

Trujillo, A. (2000). Psychotherapy with Native Americans: A view into the role of religion and spirituality. In R. P. Scott & A. E. Bergin (Eds.), *Handbook of psychotherapy and religious diversity* (pp. 445-466). Washington, DC: American Psychological Association.

Ulrich, W. L., Richards, P. S., & Bergin, A. E. (2000). Psychotherapy with Latter-day Saints. In P. S. Richards & A. E. Bergin (Eds.), *Hand-book of psychotherapy and religious diversity* (pp. 185-209). Washington, DC: American Psychological Association.

Van Hook, M., Hugen, B., & Aguilar, M. A. (Editors). (2001). *Spirituality within religious traditions in social work practice.* Pacific Grove, CA: Brooks/Cole.

Zedek, M. R. (1998). Religion and mental health from the Jewish perspective. In H. G. Koenig (Ed.), *Handbook of religion and mental health* (pp. 255-261). New York: Academic Press.